"Jesus did many other things as well" ...

Jesus Did Many Things As Well
Short Stories Out of Japan
Copyright © 2017 by Tony Schmidt

Illustrations and Cover by James Lim

All rights reserved. No part of this publication may be reproduced, distributed, or transmitted in any form or by any means, including photocopying, recording, or other electronic or mechanical methods, without the prior written permission of the author, except in the case of brief quotations embodied in critical reviews and certain other noncommercial uses permitted by copyright law.

"The title of the book is taken from the words in the Gospel of John 21:25 "Jesus did many other things as well."
The cover art is an illustrated depiction of the Odori in Sapporo, Hokkaido, where most of the stories took place.
All Scripture quotes are taken from the "New International Version."

ISBN 978-1-7751462-0-9

"Jesus did many other things as well ..."

SHORT STORIES OUT OF JAPAN

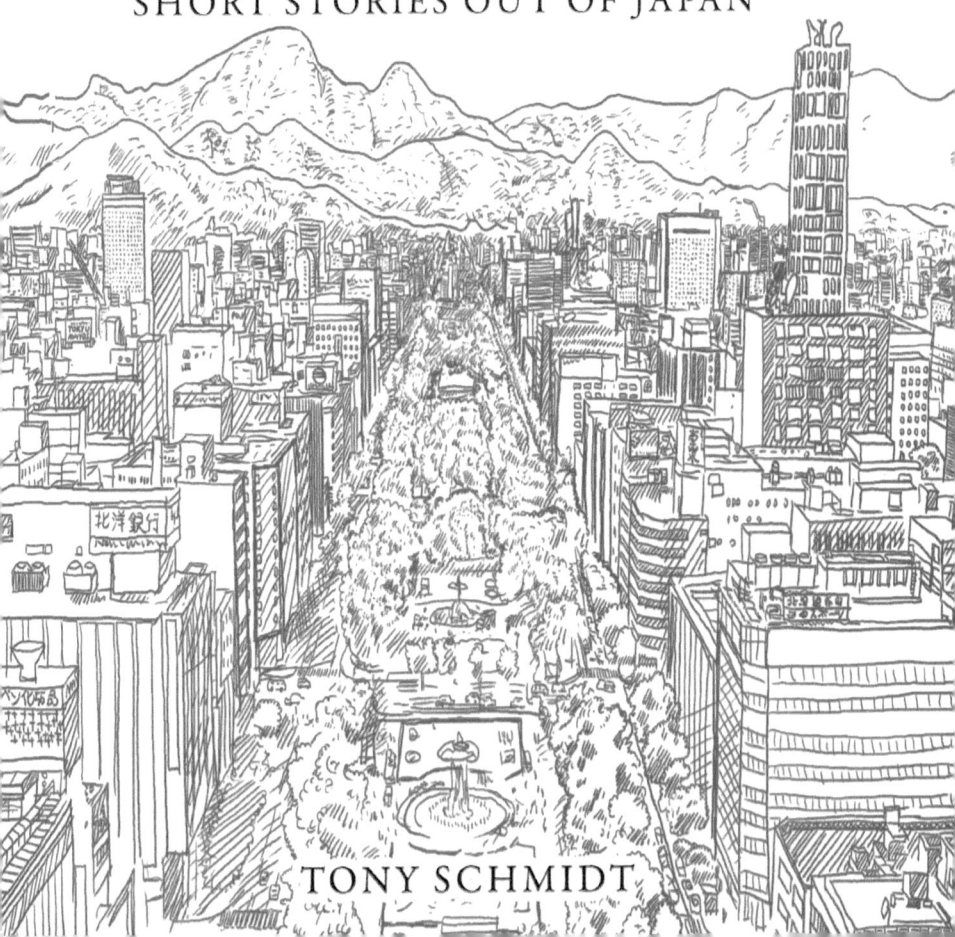

TONY SCHMIDT

CONTENTS

Preface..	7
1. What! Me a Missionary?......................	9
2. Bon Voyage......................................	17
3. A Wedding Rescued...........................	25
4. Mistaken Identity..............................	31
5. Trauma and Drama............................	37
6. Build your House on a Firm Foundation.........	43
7. Faces..	49
8. Grannies are Special...........................	55
9. Of Whom Shall I be Afraid.................	61
10. Voice from Above.............................	69
11. The Lord Opened Her Heart.............	75
12. Unforgettable Baptisms.....................	81
13. God Works in Mysterious Ways.........	89
14. Even a Shinto Priest!.........................	97
15. A Little Here, a Little There...............	103
16. Looking for the Right Location...........	109
17. You and Your Household..................	115
18. Truth Versus Harmony.....................	121
19. Running Into the Arms of God..........	127
20. Lower the Net Again!........................	133
21. A Hair-Raising Journey.....................	139

PREFACE

During our time as missionaries in Japan, a number of events stood out as being unique, interesting and often humorous. I made a note of them and always thought one day I would like to write them down more fully. With my wife Pat's support and encouragement, I have finally recorded the events for others to read. It is my hope that those who read these short stories will laugh and enjoy them, and most of all, that they will see how God is always working, often in spite of us, our weaknesses and our mistakes.

Our three precious children, Brad, Greg and Karen journeyed with us most of the way. I wanted to write these stories for them too so that they could share in the blessings as adults.

To our many faithful friends and supporters who prayed earnestly and gave generously over many years, making it possible for us to serve the Lord in Japan, we want to express our gratitude. We pray this book will give you much joy and encouragement.

Many times, in our weakness we came to understand that the "ministry of presence" is still an important ministry – just to be there often encouraged brothers and sisters in Christ in Japan to do what we could not, and so they became more fully involved in God's Kingdom work.

All the stories in this little collection are true, but names have been changed to protect the identity of those who were involved.

Special thanks to Rose Carleton and her niece, Nikki Carleton, who proofread and edited the articles, always encouraging me to move ahead with the project. I also wish to express my deep gratitude to my fellow missionaries in OMF International and precious brothers and sisters in Christ in Japan who enriched our lives and helped us to persevere to the end.

Finally, grateful thanks to our very talented friend, James Lim for enhancing the stories with his illustrations and cover design. It was very special to work with him on this project as he has been sensing a call to be a missionary to Japan since 2001 and will be moving to Osaka in September of 2017 with his family.

Enjoy the stories. We trust that as you read them, you will lift your heart to Jesus and praise HIM!

In weakness we continue to serve Him who is our strength,

Tony Schmidt
May, 2017

1. WHAT! ME, A MISSIONARY?

> *"By faith Abraham, when called to go to a place he would later receive as an inheritance, obeyed and went, even though he did not know where he was going."*
> - Hebrews 11:8

I was born in 1942 and raised in East London, South Africa. Together with my older sister, Nancy, and younger brother, Graham, I attended Sunday school at a Baptist church. My parents were not church-goers, although they came to church occasionally. When I was about 6 years old, I responded to the pastor's invitation for those who wanted to accept Jesus as Savior and Lord, to meet him in his office. When the pastor saw I was the only one there, his face fell. I was only a little child, so he advised me to come back when I was a few years older. I was disappointed because I wanted to be saved and go home as a child of God. It would be ten years before I committed myself to the Lord and was baptized at age sixteen.

Years of compromise followed. Tennis was my first love, and most of the people I played with did not make following Jesus a priority in their lives. I continued to reserve the right to live life in my own selfish way. However, deep in my heart I knew that Jesus was for real. He was the only one worthy of following. This I knew, even as I struggled to fully commit myself to Him. Finally I took the plunge, and made an announcement at my tennis club that I would no longer be available to play matches on Sunday mornings as I was a Christian, and wanted to be in church with God's family. Sure, some people I thought were my good friends mocked and laughed at me, but my heart filled with God's peace.

While studying accounting, I met Pat, who was (still is!) a lovely Christian woman. We got engaged and moved to Cape Town for work and study. A few years later, at a Youth for Christ rally, the speaker asked, "Are you sure that the work you are doing is what God wants you to do with your life?" He spoke about being a missionary and challenged us to obey God's call if it came. Although I recognized that Jesus must be both Savior and Lord, and therefore there would be no question about obeying, I felt fairly confident that I would not be called to become a missionary. Rather, it was the first question that grabbed Pat and me. We decided to set time aside to pray, asking God to give us His peace if what we were doing was His will, or to show us if He wanted to change the direction of our lives.

As we prayed, we both began to feel that God was asking us to change course. I began to think of some possibilities where my gifts might be useful to the work of the Lord. Perhaps as an administrator working at a mission hospital while doctors, nurses and evangelists administered medicine and proclaimed the Gospel? I had read stories of Christians who were called to be missionaries pleading in prayer, "Anywhere, Lord, but not Africa." I felt just the opposite. I had grown up in Africa and I wanted to serve God there if possible.

Pat and I began to knock on a few doors. At the time, we were running a Saturday night Youth for Christ club in Sea Point, Cape Town. Three of the teens were children of the Overseas Missionary Fellowship's South African Director, Don Houliston. As he travelled extensively around southern African countries, we felt he was a suitable person to ask if he knew of any openings for a Christian businessman or administrator.

Two weeks after our conversation, Don phoned to say he had just received an urgent request from OMF in Sapporo asking for an accountant/administrator to come as soon as possible. The name Sapporo did not sound African! To our horror, we learned it was a city in northern Japan! That was on the other side of the world! Upon research we discovered Sapporo had an average annual snowfall of six meters! (twenty feet). We had prayed earnestly for God's guidance. Was this from God? Or was it all just a bad coincidence? We needed more time to pray. Truth be told, I felt we needed some time to think of a good excuse why it should not be us but, rather, someone else.

We began to "count the cost" of going even for a limited time of four years. We stopped reading the evening newspaper. We prayed and fasted, seeking God's will. Isaiah 1:18 says, "'Come now, let us reason together,' says the Lord…." As we read the Bible and prayed each night, it was as if God came into our living room to talk with us. He was giving us an opportunity to put forward all our fears. What about the cold climate? We had never experienced snow before. Where do you buy clothing suitable for sub-zero temperatures in South Africa? Japanese eat raw fish and seaweed. Would there be other more edible foods in Japan? "Lord," I cried, "You know how much I love meat and potatoes!" What about the difficult language? I read somewhere that even the Devil cannot understand Japanese! I worried about financial security. I was after all an accountant! What about my pension for old age? Would there be any? One by one, I listed my fears.

One day I had a brilliant idea! I was hoping the Lord would agree. Looking at a world map, I saw that Canada is relatively close to Japan. Why not call a Canadian Christian to go to Japan? They are accustomed to the cold and snow. Economically, climatically, recreationally it all made better sense to send Canadians rather than South Africans to Japan. I almost felt the Lord might say, "What a good idea, Tony!" But He did not. Why the Lord continued to persevere with us rather than wash His hands of people of such little faith, I do not know. God is gracious and persistent. He knows our weaknesses and everything else about us too. Yet He continues to call such as us.

Meanwhile, we found our thoughts turning more and more to the Japanese people and the small Church in Japan. We found out that less than half of one percent of the population there was Christian. As we praised God in worship on Sundays, I would wonder how many of my brothers and sisters in Japan were worshiping as we were. What difficulties were they facing? How were they doing as Christians in a Buddhist/Shinto country? Were they lonely? We had so much spiritual opportunity in South Africa that it was difficult to imagine a country with so little.

I had never met a Japanese person before, and now it seemed as if God was constantly turning my eyes to Japan. Standing at traffic lights waiting to cross the street in Cape Town one day, I asked an Asian man where he was from. "From Japan," he replied. I walked into a company office to audit their financial books, and while waiting at the reception desk I noticed a calendar on the wall. It was a picture of a lovely city. As I peered more closely, I discovered it was Sapporo! Doing night evangelism one weekend, we came upon some Japanese sailors in a bar. Suddenly Japan seemed everywhere!

One Sunday in March 1971, our pastor preached from Hebrews 11:8: "By faith Abraham, when called to go to a place he would later receive as an inheritance, obeyed and went, even though he did not know where he was going." Abraham did not know where God was going to lead him. We knew where we would go! But Abraham trusted God. Should I not trust Him too? I had been given an even greater knowledge of God than Abraham had. I knew about God's plan of salvation. I knew about the death and resurrection of the Lord Jesus Christ. He who gave His life for me can surely be trusted. Convicted, embarrassed, repentant and joyful that God had brought us to the point of being willing to go where He was leading us, we decided together that we would follow the Lord to Sapporo, Japan.

Looking back on our lives, Pat and I continually give thanks to God for His guidance, and for not giving up on two of His fear-filled children.

2. BON VOYAGE!

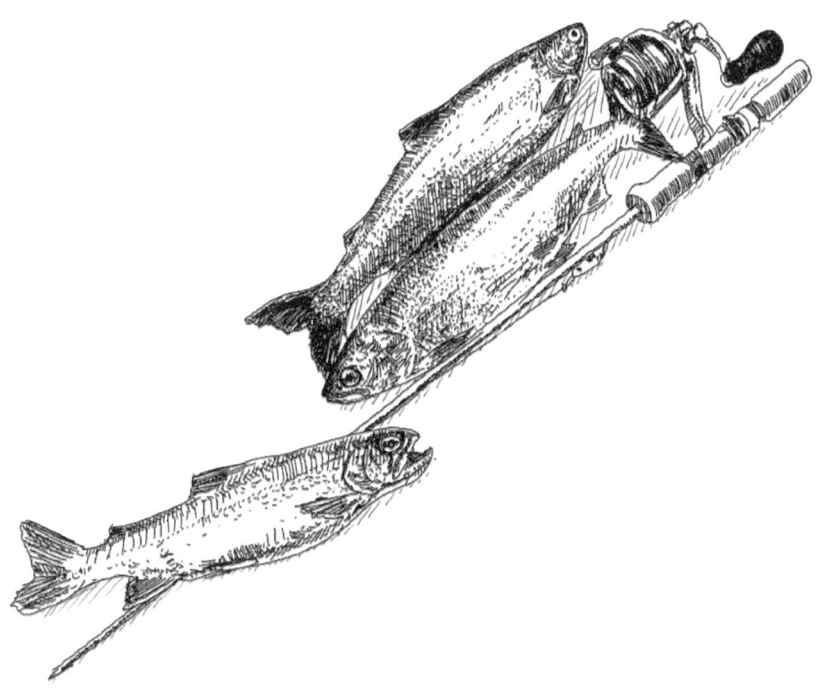

"God is our refuge and strength, an ever-present help in trouble. Therefore we will not fear, though the earth give way, and the mountains fall into the heart of the sea, though its waters roar and foam and the mountains quake with their surging."
- Psalm 46: 1-3

In 1853 Hudson Taylor, founder of the China Inland Mission, later known as OMF International, sailed on the "good ship" Dumfries to China. It took 156 days to get there! Since the 1960s, missionaries generally fly to distant locations. However, in 1975, the OMF Director in South Africa requested that we return to Japan by ship rather than fly, as it would be much less expensive. Mission finances were always quite tight, but at that time they were even tighter than usual. So we agreed to go by ship from South Africa to Japan. It was to be our first term as long-term missionaries.

We found out that the voyage would take about 35 days of sailing from Cape Town to Yokohama, Japan via Port Elizabeth, Hong Kong, Taiwan (Port of Keelung); and from there through three different ports in Japan – Shimonoseki, Nagoya and Yokohama. From Yokohama we would go by ferry to Hokkaido and then on to Sapporo, where we were due to study Japanese for a year and a half. Our ship was the SA Shipper, a cargo vessel carrying fish meal to Japan. Being the oldest vessel in the South African Merchant Navy, it was going to be scrapped, and this would be its last trip. At first it all sounded exciting, but when we thought about our two small boys (ages two and a half and thirteen months), we felt anxious about the lack of adequate medical care available. We heard that a young officer who had taken a crash course in general first aid was the designated Medical Officer. This did nothing to alleviate our fears! However, a few days before the sailing date, the OMF Director told us with a huge smile that of the nine passengers on board, two "happened" to be qualified medical doctors. God is good!

The first night sailing around the Cape Peninsula, we encountered the huge swells of the infamous "Cape Rollers." Pat and I took turns with our heads in the toilet. Fortunately our boys slept right through the night. During the day we would spend time on deck studying our Japanese language textbooks while the children played nearby. There was no railing around the deck, only ropes, which would not prevent a child from falling overboard. We found some spare rope to tie around the boys' waists and anchor them to a pole so we didn't have to watch them every moment. What a relief! They happily played in the sand of several fire boxes that we had gathered together.

While in port at Port Elizabeth, I asked the Captain for permission to conduct a Bible study in the passenger lounge. A notice advertising the weekly meeting was pinned on the door of the bar. The first Sunday night all seven passengers, the Captain, First Engineer and Officers attended. I had to arrange a separate meeting for the rest of the crew. At some time during the first meeting, I said that even if Hitler had repented, God in His grace would have forgiven him. The Chief Engineer responded that if that were so, he would live life as he pleased and then shortly before he died, he would repent and be saved. I commented that the problem is we don't know when we will die. The Chief Engineer assured me that everyone has a premonition of their death, so there would always be time to repent. At this point the Captain stated that he himself believed what the Bible taught, but he knew he was not living in accordance to the Word of God. The Chief Engineer, possibly fearing that he was about to lose his drinking partner, strongly tried to dissuade the Captain. The rest of us looked on, embarrassed by their open disagreement.

Two weeks after the first Bible Study, the Captain, a lady passenger and the Chief Engineer were standing at the bar enjoying a drink before dinner. Suddenly the Captain put his arm out towards her and fell over. He had a sudden heart attack and was not able to recover, despite the immediate attention given by the two doctors on board. The Captain, according to his wishes, was buried at sea after permission was obtained by radio from his wife in South Africa. I was asked to give a short memorial service and after that, according to each person's background, I was addressed as Padre, Father, Priest or Reverend!

The Chief Engineer came to the subsequent Sunday evening Bible studies and listened quietly. Sadly though, towards the end of our voyage he regained some of his old bravado and began opposing what the Bible taught. I felt comforted that the Captain had at least made a confession of belief, although he did not have much time to demonstrate it publicly. A replacement captain was flown in from Ireland and he joined us just off Singapore.

Bible studies for the rest of the crew were conducted at the stern of the ship. The motion of bobbing up and down is far worse at the stern. Opening my Bible, I was about to start the first study when one of the crew pulled out a large knife. He was very angry, and I wondered what he had against the Bible! However, it turned out he was upset with another crew member who had reported on him. He wanted to stab that person, not me! It took quite a while to calm him down, but we did eventually do the first study together. Over time the man asked questions indicating his interest, but I am not aware of his making a commitment to follow Jesus.

One Sunday night during the Bible study for passengers and officers, we had a discussion about the meaning of sin. Several people denied that they were sinners, as they insisted they did not do anything so bad that it would warrant that label. However, when they understood that even our unrighteous thoughts are regarded as sin, the Medical Officer blurted, "Well then, everyone is a sinner!" No one opposed that statement, but somehow they still felt their sins did not require a Savior to die for them. That was too extreme an assessment, they said.

During the long trip, we got to know the officers and some of the crew well. One day they asked if I would like to see the engine room. I eagerly agreed. We descended by ladder into the depths. The noise of the engines was loud. It was interesting to see all the machinery that pushed the ship along its course, but the most startling sight was a crew member fishing in a trough of water coming from the area of the propellers. Apparently some fish were sucked in via the gap where the propeller shaft went through the ship's hull. Next to the man's small fishing rod lay two fish. As I watched, he pulled out a third fish! I was amazed, but they assured me the ship would not sink from this small intake of water. The fish would be prepared for dinner that night. "Enjoy," they said. That night we ate the fish, deliciously prepared. Everybody was laughing because word had got around that the Padre had swallowed the bait – hook, line and sinker! The fish had been taken from the freezer and laid next to our fisherman friend so that he could catch an even bigger "fish!"

After three weeks at sea, we landed at Hong Kong. We watched the stevedores come on board and were horrified to see them spit into the sandboxes that our children had played in! They had probably been used as spittoons by the stevedores over decades. We hastily removed the boys' little cars and washed them thoroughly, and scrubbed the boys' hands and under their fingernails too! The fact that no one got sick was surely God's protection. Needless to say, the boys were upset that their favorite play-place was now out of bounds!

When we docked at Keelung, Taiwan, we had a few days in port. I decided it would be interesting to take a train to see Taipei City. The taxi driver could not speak any English and my Taiwanese was non-existent, so I made some train-like noises to give him an idea of where I wanted to go. He took me to a nightclub, pointing upstairs with a smile on his face! When I shook my head in refusal, he then took me to the police station. The taxi driver accompanied me in, but none of the police officers could figure out what I was doing there. Neither could I!

Eventually an older man, more senior in rank, came out of his office to join the discussion. He wrote a Chinese character and enquired if I understood the meaning. In Japanese I said "Higashi," which means east, because Japanese and Chinese characters are mostly the same. Straightaway he asked me in Japanese my reason for being in the police station. We were communicating in Japanese, much to the amusement of the younger policemen in the office! The older policeman was enjoying our talk, which showed that he was still one up over the younger men. He could speak Japanese because of Japan's occupation of Taiwan which lasted 50 years, to the end of the Second World War. Turning to the taxi driver, he gave instructions to take me to the railway station, and from there I went on my way to Taipei City.

After 35 days on board the ship and a ferry, we were relieved to be back in Hokkaido. The Lord had safely brought us to our destination, through some terrifying storms where the swells looked like mountains and the troughs like deep valleys. At times we could not see the sky – only the angry, turbulent, dark sea. During one storm the ship's engines had to be stopped, and we bobbed around in huge swells for three days. I was convinced we were all going to die. Picking up our two boys, we sang, "The Lord your God in the midst of you is mighty, is mighty…." After singing to the boys, we felt much better, trusting the Lord to take us safely to Japan.

Before we finally disembarked, one of the doctors said to me, "You wouldn't give me that Bible, would you?" I had walked the streets of Cape Town looking for a leather-bound Bible which would fit into my jacket pocket. I was delighted to have found exactly what I was looking for and was thankful to have it always with me. Now I was being asked to give it away! However, looking at the doctor, who often had been quite critical of my talks, I said I would be happy to give it to him provided he would read it. A month after we arrived in Japan, we got a letter from his wife to say that he had died suddenly – just like the Captain! I was so grateful that I had parted with my precious Bible, giving the doctor two months to read it before he went to meet his Maker. It really had been a memorable voyage!

3. A WEDDING RESCUED

"A wedding took place at Cana in Galilee. ...When the wine was gone, Jesus' mother said to him, "They have no more wine." ...Jesus said to the servants, "Fill the jars with water"... and the master of the banquet tasted the water that had been turned into wine."
- John 2: 1-9

A handsome young man named Michito began attending the church where Laura, an American single missionary, was serving. It was an exciting time when Michito believed and was baptized. Their relationship blossomed into love, and they announced their engagement to be married. Everyone at church was very happy, but Michito's father was dead against the proposed marriage on two accounts – (1) his son was going to marry a foreigner and (2) she was a Christian. It was bad enough that his son had become a Christian, but now it would seem that any future offspring would become Christians as well!

Many people in Japan feel that to become a Christian is to be no longer fully Japanese. In Japanese thinking, the spirits of the ancestors are still very much part of the present family and filial piety is a highly prized virtue. Many people believe that their spirit's wellbeing after death depends on how religiously their offspring carry out their duties of prayer and offering rice and drink to the spirits of the deceased ancestors at the family Buddhist altar. To faithfully attend to this altar is seen as an honorable act of filial piety. Parents and grandparents often feel abandoned and alarmed at what appears to them to be the ingratitude of offspring who refuse to perform their filial duties when they become Christians.

For these reasons Michito's father was very upset. He announced that if the wedding was to go ahead as planned he would disown his son, cut him off from the family inheritance and refuse to go to the wedding.

Despite this threat, Michito and Laura decided to proceed with their wedding plans. Because her father was unable to come to Japan for the wedding, Laura asked me to walk her down the aisle on her wedding day to give her away to her husband-to-be. Feeling honored, I quickly agreed, and then realized that I would also be expected to give a speech in Japanese on behalf of Laura's family at the reception! Such speeches have to be given using a highly polite form of Japanese with which I was not very familiar.

In preparing the speech, I became more aware of Michito's family's feelings. The father was adamantly opposed, but the other family members were caught up in the joy of the coming wedding on the one hand, and the anger of Michito's father on the other. There was great tension in the family.

At that time I was still studying at the Japanese Language School in Sapporo and I was in the process of reading and studying the Prodigal Son (Houtou Musuko) story. Learning new words and trying to get my tongue to pronounce them acceptably was always a challenge and now this, my first wedding speech, seemed to be full of difficult new words to pronounce and remember!

Soon the great day of the wedding dawned. On the way to the church, I had my speech next to me on the passenger seat. At every traffic light I would once again quickly scan my script before driving off. At one traffic light I was a bit slow to brake and gently bumped into the back of a bus. The driver did not bother to check, but all the passengers in the back seat turned around to look at who had bumped the bus. My stress level spiked! I was still sitting in the car bowing my apologies as the bus pulled away.

Once I arrived at the church I went over to greet Michito's very anxious-looking family members. His father had reluctantly agreed to attend the wedding at the last minute, and now no one knew what to expect from him. I tried to encourage Laura to relax and enjoy her wedding day and then walked her down the aisle to the waiting groom. As I sat through the wedding service I found myself praying and trying to memorize my speech rather than listening to what was being said.

At the reception, I noticed that none of the guests at Michito's family table were eating or talking. Everyone was looking furtively at the father, hoping he would at least pretend to look happy. He would not. It promised to be a very dismal wedding reception.

The time of reckoning arrived. I was called upon to give my congratulatory speech. Amongst the guests were family members, friends of the bride and the groom, church members, language school teachers and fellow missionaries. I felt fairly comfortable with the opening paragraph of my speech. "I won't have to read every word of the first paragraph," I thought. Smiling at the guests, I boldly opened my mouth and started to speak. I had not gone far before I realized that there was a lot of whispering and chuckling going on. Michito's father raised his eyes. Looking at me, he started to smile! Then he erupted with laughter. At this, the other family members began to laugh with him. This prompted many other guests to start laughing too! The atmosphere took on a lighter note. Everyone except me seemed to be enjoying a good joke. I suspected that I had made a grammatical error but in my panicky state I did not realize the mistake I had made. I finally got through the speech and sat down, relieved that it was over.

After the reception quite a few missionaries and Japanese said they admired my nerve to crack a joke like that. Apparently I had addressed the couple as "bride and prodigal son" – I had called the groom "Houtou Musuko" instead of "Hanamuko." No wonder Michito's father had looked upon me with favor. He thought he had found a like-minded person! The word prodigal described how he felt about his son! Despite all the congratulations and expressions of admiration received due to my unintended joke, I felt deeply ashamed that I had embarrassed my friend Michito and his bride on their special day. When I apologized to them later, they told me that they thought I had done that on purpose to break the tension!

Long ago Jesus also attended a wedding. A tense situation arose when the wine ran out. The bridal couple would have been greatly embarrassed, but Jesus rescued them from that predicament by turning water into wine.

As my wife and I drove home, we felt that Jesus had rescued the wedding by letting me make that error in order to bring blessing and happiness to the couple, as well as many others. That would be just like Jesus!

Michito and Laura moved away from Sapporo so it was a year or two later when we heard the good news that a baby boy was born to them. They told us that nobody was more proud of their boy than Michito's father, who had reinstated his son, accepted his daughter-in-law, and was a very happy grandfather!

4. MISTAKEN IDENTITY

> *"A cheerful heart is good medicine..."*
> - Proverbs 17:22

As a young couple, we were in the process of adjusting from a warm Southern Hemisphere country to the cold climate of the island of Hokkaido, northern Japan. Seen from the southern tip of Africa, where we had come from, Hokkaido appears awfully close to the North Pole. It certainly felt like the North Pole to us! Every year approximately six meters (twenty feet) of snow falls. Fortunately, it is dry snow which can be brushed off your head or clothing without leaving any dampness.

The contrasts of the seasons are distinct and magnificent. The changing colors of leaves in the autumn take one's breath away. Varied greens give way to yellow, orange, rustic brown and red. Winter has its own special beauty – especially if you like white! During the long winter season, there are frequent days of bright sunshine with clear blue skies. Walking in the snow at night with a full moon shining is an unforgettable experience. Although less than 1% of the population are Christian, I think the Lord has given the Japanese people an emphatic witness of His handiwork through the wonderful changing seasons. Year after year, season after season, nature testifies to the magnificence of God's creation. Japanese people do indeed love nature, but most have yet to meet the Creator of it all.

Prior to coming to Japan in 1971, my wife and I were under the impression that all Japanese look remarkably alike. There was a uniformity of dress and everyone had black hair and brown eyes, so this tended to reinforce our mistaken impression. However, we soon realized that, although there are similarities in appearance, everyone is unique.

Through the following incident, we began to understand that, to some of our Japanese friends all Caucasians also look alike!

One day on my way back from town, I popped into our local electric appliance store. I had been there previously with my wife, trying to get a toaster element repaired. The shop assistant had looked really puzzled as I tried to tell him what I wanted. He kept showing me new toasters and, as I shook my head, he would show me another. I was hugging and pointing to my own toaster, which only required an element to be replaced. Eventually, after much talking and gesticulating, I realized that in Japan, when something no longer works, you dispose of it and buy a new one.

As I was leaving the store, the shop assistant dropped a bombshell. He said my wife had just been in and bought a new washing machine. I smiled and said it could not have been my wife. We had not even spoken about buying a new washing machine. However, he assured me it was my wife. I nearly freaked out when he told me how much it had cost. We were not able to afford the luxury of a new washing machine, let alone an expensive one. Pat and I had always discussed and prayed together about big purchases. What could have got into her head, I wondered, that she would do something so rash? This was a huge financial outlay and it should have been carefully prayed about and thought through before making the decision to buy!

I hurried out of the store after the man insisted there was no mistake – it was my wife who had already paid for the washing machine. I grew more annoyed with every step towards home. I hardly greeted my sweet wife when I opened the door. My eyes flitted around to find the "culprit" that had taken up residence in our small apartment. I demanded to know where she had hidden the washing machine. She probably wanted to give me a "nice surprise", I reasoned.

Now it was my wife's turn to regard me anxiously, as I was behaving so out of character. *Has he been studying too hard or eating too much pickled radish?* she wondered. *Surely he knows we would discuss and pray about such a major purchase before making a decision. What on earth has got into him?*

A quick search of our one-bedroom apartment revealed no new washing machine. As we both calmed down, we came to the conclusion that the appliance shop assistant had indeed been mistaken. My shaken confidence in my wife was restored and we were still financially solvent!

The mystery was cleared up later when our American friends visited us and, amongst other things, told us they had bought a wonderful new washing machine! I was very glad it was them and not us, as our washing machine was still doing fine. My friend's wife did not look the least bit like mine! However, quite understandably, to the Japanese shop assistant these two foreign ladies had looked exactly the same.

This incident helped me to understand at an early stage of my missionary career the following life principles:

1. Assumptions should not be made before all the facts are examined.
2. Do not worry over things that may never happen.
3. Remember to give your wife the credit she deserves.
4. Never lose your sense of humor.
5. Carry a photo of your wife in your wallet!

5. TRAUMA AND DRAMA

"Oh, that I had the wings of a dove! I would fly away and be at rest."
- Psalm 55:6

These words from Psalm 55:6 have special significance for every new missionary struggling to get a grasp of the Japanese language. Most students studying Japanese at times want to fly away to get relief from the continual stress of struggling to read, write and speak Japanese. A gifted linguist among the new recruits may cause less gifted ones to want to fly away even sooner, as we inevitably get caught in the trap of comparing ourselves with others.

The first few weeks of excitement for the new missionary soon turn into a tedious, frustrating, heartbreaking time as we see little progress despite much effort and prayers for a quick miracle to aid us in bringing the Gospel to Japan. My own prayers grew even more earnest as language tests drew near, but sometimes after the tests my teachers looked at me as if I had not prayed sufficiently! However, disappointment began to verge on pride, or perhaps self-satisfaction, when a new batch of missionary recruits arrived at Language School, enviously regarding us "oldies" as being fluent in Japanese because we had learned a few sentences well.

Lack of language is not always a disadvantage – at least not in the early months, as shown by the following incident. We were living in an old house opposite the Language School. The water from our well had a strange taste. Therefore, without my noticing it, my liquid intake over a period of time was grossly insufficient. During language study one day, I experienced an excruciating pain in my stomach. My teacher observed that my face had turned "blue" (equivalent to pale in English). I didn't know which way to sit on my chair. Every position was extremely painful. Someone suggested I might have a kidney stone, so the Language Coordinator kindly drove me to the Angel Hospital.

As soon as we entered the hospital parking lot, even before the car was parked, I headed for the reception desk. A long line of patients were waiting their turn. Seeing the agony on my face, a nurse kindly enquired what my trouble was. Either through lack of language or divine providence, I said "*Shinzo* (heart)" instead of "*Jinzo* (kidney)". The sudden change of her expression from calmness to alarm reminded me of my language teachers' faces when on occasion I had made a hash of their language in class! The now panic-stricken nurse rushed me to the head of the line shouting, "*Shinzo! Shinzo!*" People hurriedly made way, giving me concerned looks as I was ushered in ahead of everyone else to see the doctor. I was soon stretched out on a bed with various complicated-looking wires attached to my body.

The doctor began to examine my chest but I told him the pain was lower down, on the side of my stomach. Puzzled at first, he suddenly began laughing, saying something to the nurses, who also burst out laughing. I was not amused, as I felt people should not laugh at a man who was in agony! It was indeed diagnosed as a kidney stone, and together with the medication, the doctor said I should drink lots of liquids and take frequent hot baths to sweat it out. My fear subsided as I realized it was not a life-threatening condition, even though the pain was still intense. The many patients still waiting in line were surprised to see me walking out unattended by any concerned nurses, who were still chuckling among themselves behind the curtains. I felt somewhat consoled that a little fun had come into their lives at my expense!

After a week at home nearly drowning from all the liquids I had to drink, I heard a ping as the kidney stone passed through my system and landed in the potty. I was disappointed that I was barely able to see the stone it was so small. I thought it would definitely be the size of a small marble, judging from the pain it had caused! It was a relief to be free of physical pain, but the pain of continued language learning persisted. As my language improved, I knew I could not count on such an error to get me to the head of the line should there be another emergency! Since that time, my fluid intake has increased in accordance with doctors' instructions. No more kidney stones to this day!

While we were in language study, another young couple were experiencing a difficult time with frequent colds and slow progress in the language. One day as Jean was hanging out her laundry, she accidently stepped on the rake her husband had forgotten to put away. The handle of the rake whipped up, hitting her in the face. In an effort to cheer up her drooping spirits, she decided to bake some cookies. The gas oven would not light despite repeated attempts to turn the ignition knob. Unfamiliar with gas appliances, she opened the oven door and reached in with a lighted match to manually light the oven. There was a loud bang as a whoosh of hot air and flames billowed out, singeing her eyebrows and hair. Thoroughly discouraged, she phoned the mission Superintendent, who sympathetically booked them off for a few days of rest and refreshment at the Lake Doya holiday home.

The holiday home was set in a beautiful area near an emerald-colored lake surrounded by trees. Isolated and quiet, it was the ideal place just to rest and relax. There was no need to wear a watch. When on holiday, time stands still until you have to pack to return home, wondering why the time flew by so fast. There was no phone to disturb the peace. This should be the ideal place to restore shattered nerves and singed eyebrows.

Jean is a gentle, nature-loving person who loved collecting pretty leaves for arrangements. Taking a basket, she went out to collect some colorful autumn leaves. As she wandered amongst the bushes to get the ones she wanted, she suddenly felt her face starting to burn. When she returned home, her husband took one look at her red, swollen face and started to pack up. By the time they arrived back in Sapporo, Jean's face had swollen to such an extent she could barely see. She was immediately admitted to hospital. The doctor booked her off for a week to recover from her encounter with poison ivy. Oh, for the wings of a dove!

Despite all the trauma and drama that comes to new missionaries who must adjust to different ways of living, most feel that the tough experiences during those initial language- and culture-learning days stand them in good stead to handle the trials that lie ahead. The blessing of being able to continue serving the Lord makes them glad they did not fly away on the wings of a dove.

6. BUILD YOUR HOUSE ON A FIRM FOUNDATION

The wise man built his house upon the Rock.
- Matthew 7:24

Our first church planting designation after graduating from language school in 1976 was to work in a southern suburb of Sapporo City in Hokkaido. People often ask, "How long did it take you to learn to speak Japanese?" I always truthfully reply, "Thirty-three years and counting!"

While at language school, we receive much encouragement from everyone who hears us speaking Japanese. "My, you are nearly fluent," they say encouragingly. Later on as expectations increase there is much sucking in of breath, heads dropping to a slightly sideways slant (equivalent to a westerner's raised eyebrows) and sometimes completely blank looks. Missionaries must be both humble and tough. Otherwise we could find ourselves on a plane heading home earlier than our supporters expected to see us.

As a young family with two pre-school boys and a baby on the way, we eagerly looked forward to our first assignment as church planting missionaries. First we had to find an affordable apartment or house. We and the few believers – three adults and three teenagers – could find nothing suitable. We were prepared to live quite simply, so it was not a matter of being too fussy. Mr. Tanaka, the only man among the nucleus of believers, owned a piece of land nearby on which he decided to build a house which he would then rent to us. Prior to graduation from Language School, we received an invitation to attend the dedication of the building before the roofing and flooring were completed. I was delighted to attend, along with the senior missionary couple from a nearby church who would be supervising us.

Setting out after morning classes were over, I arrived at Mr. Tanaka's house, a short distance from where our future home was located. Mr. Tanaka asked me to carry some hymnbooks and Bibles to the site, a three-minute walk away. As we walked, he told me that the senior missionaries were not able to be present at the ceremony that day. "Well, then who will be leading the dedication ceremony and bringing the message?" I enquired. Mr. Tanaka looked vaguely surprised and calmly replied, "You will be doing it." I hoped it was a joke. It was not!

At that point I should have bolted for the bus stop, but my legs felt too weak to carry me. Totally aghast, I began to pray fervently. Was it possible for His second coming to occur before the ceremony started? Despite my desperate prayers, it did not. Fortunately for everyone, including myself, I had just done a little reading in Japanese on Jesus' parable about two men. One had built his house on the rock and the other one built his on the sand. In my panic during the minute-and-a-half preparation time available to me, I could not find the passage in the Bible. (I may even have attempted to find it in the Old Testament!) I had to speak in Japanese from my memory of the passage in English.

Seven carpenters and several believers were standing in a circle in the kitchen area when we arrived. The kitchen floor had been completed, but in other rooms one could see the foundation of the house. Never have I been less excited about moving into a new home. It should have been an exhilarating experience, but I was feeling depressed over the debacle that was about to unfold with me in the starring role.

The Japanese word for kitchen is *daidokoro* and the word for foundation is *dodai*. Trying to look as confident as I could whilst doing my level best to stop my legs from shaking, I commenced the ceremony. After a hymn and a prayer (in addition to my own silent, pleading prayers) I emphasized how important it was to have a good foundation for a building. I hoped the carpenters did not think I was questioning their workmanship. In my best Japanese (which probably came over in a form they had never heard before!) I moved on to talk about the need of a good foundation for life. Observing the carpenters' faces as I spoke, it seemed to me that nothing I said was being understood. Their faces registered nothing at all.

Then a thought hit me. Perhaps I was using the wrong word for foundation! Maybe the word was *daido*, not *dodai*. We were standing in the *daidokoro* (kitchen) which by many people would be considered the main area of the building. After all, the kitchen was the place where food would be prepared, so one could think of it as a kind of foundation for the entire building!

I reasoned that I could continue as I was, talking about the *dodai*, or use *daido* instead. (I later learned there is no such word!) I would either be completely wrong or absolutely correct. The blank faces of the carpenters convinced me I had been using the wrong word for foundation, so as subtly as I could, I changed to *daido*, expecting their faces to light up with understanding. Nothing changed! Their faces remained impassive. Finally, after exhausting my Japanese vocabulary (and my hearers and myself too!), I brought the service to a close by asking Mr. Tanaka to pray. The Dedication Ceremony was over. Presents were given to the carpenters, and we all went home after much bowing and thanking the carpenters for their good work thus far. My bowing was with a mixture of thanks and an apology for murdering their language.

The carpenters must have done a good job because our family lived there happily for a few years. Thirty years later, the building is still standing and looking in good condition. In fact, the present Japanese pastor is living there. I omitted to tell you that during the Dedication of the Building Ceremony, we buried a Bible in a glass container in the sand right under the staircase. The house was figuratively and nearly literally built upon the rock of God's Word.

It must be mentioned that this story is a picture of the grace extended to us so often by Japanese people as we struggled to speak their language. Mr. Tanaka never mentioned my huge mistake. In fact, he seemed to be unaware of it. Such is true grace.

By the way, are you building your house on the Rock?

7. FACES

"When Moses came down from Mount Sinai with the two tablets of the Testimony in his hands, he was not aware that his face was radiant, because he had spoken with the Lord."
- Exodus 34: 29.

Faces are fascinating. In Japanese culture it is etiquette not to cause a person to lose face. It is better to leave room for maneuverability so that your adversary can save face and be given a discreet opportunity to make an apology. Thus a person's reputation is not harmed by shaming him with a "checkmate" move. Quite possibly that person may adopt a more friendly attitude in recognition of the kindness shown him.

Displaying emotions of disappointment, anger or frustration is viewed as weakness in a person's character. Westerners are often confused by the stoic expression on the face of a Japanese person. Words, not facial expressions, are relied upon to convey meaning. For example, when receiving a gift, many Japanese would wait for an opportune time to open the present privately rather than in the presence of the giver, lest their faces show disappointment or not enough pleasure to fit the occasion.

When Moses came down from Mount Sinai after talking with God, he was not aware that his radiant face disclosed that He had been in the presence of Almighty God. This is the kind of face that every Christian desires – a face that radiates the warmth of God after spending time in His presence. Sometimes hidden sins or a lack of appreciation or love for God, His children or our neighbors prevent us from drawing close to God.

In one of our early church planting assignments, there were two teenage sisters, Misa and Yurika. Misa was a Christian but not a very committed one. She frequently turned up late for church, even though she lived just a few minutes away. She often quarreled with her younger sister, Yurika, which did nothing to commend her faith to her family. However, she attended church services regularly and prayed for her sister's salvation. Sometimes Yurika would attend youth-focused outreaches and occasionally even came to a Sunday worship service. But basically she remained resistant to all attempts to explain the Gospel. Yurika always had a dark countenance. She seemed to be enveloped by an invisible dark cloud.

One day as I was preparing my sermon and looking over the church bulletin, I heard footsteps as someone entered the room. Barely glancing up, I said, "*Ohayo gozaimasu* (good morning)," to which I heard a gentle response. Looking up, I saw a face glowing with joy. It was Yurika! Her face was glowing and she looked transformed. I had never seen such a dramatic change in a person's face. Yurika had met Jesus. Her heart had been changed, and her radiant face bore witness of her new faith in the Lord. Apparently she had been reading the Bible quietly in her room, so neither her sister nor anyone else knew that behind that resistant face was a soul searching for meaning in life. Perhaps it was pride that kept her from seeking assistance. I'm not sure, but one thing was sure, Yurika had been born again! Her face had changed! Misa and Yurika became loving sisters and supportive of each other. Their mother was impressed with the change in her two daughters and was ultimately drawn to their Savior too.

At another church, a young missionary couple was assigned to work with us. The church was located on a fairly busy road with many people driving past but few coming in. One man who did stop to enquire was Mr. Murata. He was in a desperate state, as his business was failing, making it difficult to pay his debts. One of his sons was a special needs child who needed a lot of extra care. Added to this, his wife was critical of how he was handling his life and business. Mr. Murata was at the end of his tether and thought he would have to go to a psychiatrist or to a church to seek help. He thought the church was a possible source of help because he drove past it every day, and one day he noticed the young missionary getting into his car with a big smile on his face. That smile kindled a longing in Mr. Murata's heart as he wondered whether he would ever be able to smile again. That smile gave him hope, and the courage to enter the church.

I distinctly remember the day he hesitantly entered the church and asked if it was OK for a person who wasn't a Christian to attend. He came regularly from the word go. He didn't understand much of what was taking place during the service, but he read many of the books in the church library. He was also reading a lot about faith in Jesus via the internet. Because he was not busy during the day, we did a personal Bible study each week, sometimes for two hours at a time. He started feeling more at ease with Christians and began to attend the mid-week prayer meeting.

It was during an Alpha course that Mr. Murata took courage and committed his life to Christ. He was baptized and, although no one from his family came to witness the celebration, Mr. Murata's face beamed with joy. Since then, his warm smile has blessed the members of the church and welcomed many newcomers as they ventured in.

Isn't it amazing that it was a smile that brought Mr. Murata to church? A moment earlier or later and he would not have seen the smile that so touched his heart.

When we are walking obediently with God, delighting in His presence, talking to Him as a man speaks with his friend, we may be surprised to learn to whom God will speak through a face made radiant by His love.

8. GRANNIES ARE SPECIAL

> *"Even to your old age and gray hairs I am he,*
> *I am he who will sustain you."*
> - Isaiah 46:4

When new missionaries first arrive in Japan, they spend two years and two months learning how to speak, read and write Japanese. For most people it is a hard grind during which pride and do-it-yourself mentalities are challenged. Fervent prayer, hard work and a sense of humor are necessary. It is a humbling time, but encouragements do come – such as recognizing a word or two while listening to a long sermon while sitting on a hard chair with feet in slippers that are far too small! (In Japan, it's still customary in smaller churches to take off your shoes and slip on the provided slippers when you enter.) Even just making the right sound at the right time while singing a hymn with the congregation can be an exhilarating experience. Initially, attending church was an endurance test, but little by little things got better, until one day I was suddenly asked to pray in Japanese. That was one time I came close to having a heart attack. Maybe only the Lord knew what I was praying about that day! After that, I learned to be prepared by carrying a short prayer in Japanese in my back pocket to be used in emergencies.

Even during those early days when most of what I heard was *non comprehendo*, I always felt my heart warmed as we sang the doxology. I knew that I was in the right place worshipping the Lord with my brothers and sisters in Christ in Japan. Every Sunday as I approached the church building, a little old granny clad in a kimono would graciously greet me outside the church. Placing her hands together, she would bow and welcome me. Her warm welcome was something I looked forward to each week. I often wondered if she was the Lord in disguise!

Because foreigners in Hokkaido were rare in the early '70s, we frequently received looks of utter amazement as we travelled around. Babies used to burst into tears when I looked at them, which did nothing for my already battered self image! The words "*Gaijin, gaijin* (foreigner, foreigner)" followed us everywhere. One man even fell off his bike in shock when he suddenly caught sight of my wife pushing our son in a stroller. So it was a privilege to be warmly greeted by that special granny at church each week.

One day when I went to town I needed to post a letter. The letter box had two slots with instructions written only in Japanese, which I could not decipher. I asked a lady passing by to help me, but she hurriedly waved her hand in front of her face saying, "I don't speak English." I had spoken Japanese, but looking at my face she assumed it was English! Perhaps I should ask a man, I reasoned. The next "victim" actually jumped off the sidewalk into the street and then back on the sidewalk beyond me as he saw me approach. Do I look like I have leprosy or something? I wondered, feeling irritated. Finally, I approached three schoolgirls walking towards me. With much giggling, they indicated the appropriate slot for my letter to South Africa.

Still feeling a bit down, I walked to the bus stop and boarded a bus which I assumed was the right one. The changing scenery I saw as we travelled along soon made me realize I was going to a different destination. I had misread the characters on the front of the bus. I jumped off and began to walk in the general direction of my home, my umbrella pulled down over my face for protection against the wind and snow.

Now and then I would lift the umbrella to check my way. As I walked along, still heavy-hearted, tired, and not a little irritated, I became aware of a pair of shoes approaching me. A lady not able to see my face said, "Excuse me."

As many people had been surprised at seeing a foreigner's face, I thought I would be naughty and have a bit of fun. Abruptly lifting my umbrella and looking into her eyes I said, "Yes," expecting her to take off in fright.

Instead the lady, who was a granny, calmly looked back at me and asked if I knew the way to the local Co-op store. I did, and I was delighted to have a normal conversation with a stranger. I offered to walk her there, but she said, "Just tell me. I will find it." Summoning up all the Japanese I knew (interspersed with a few as yet undiscovered words, no doubt!), I explained where the Co-op was and she set off in the right direction. I was greatly encouraged after our conversation and continued my journey home walking at least a few centimeters above the snow. I was renewed in my desire to learn this language, no matter how difficult it would be!

The Lord knows how to encourage His children at the right time. Was it the Lord disguised as a granny again? It may have been Him. So pay careful attention when you talk with a granny. You never know who she may really be!

9. OF WHOM SHALL I BE AFRAID?

*"The Lord is my light and my salvation – whom shall I fear?
The Lord is the stronghold of my life – of whom shall I be afraid?"*
- Psalm 27:1

The little pioneer church where we were working was growing slowly. There was a need for more workers, but the laborers were few. Furthermore, the few believers all seemed to be extremely busy, either because they had a job or were looking after babies and young children. (Looking after children is a very demanding job, to which any parent or grandparent who has looked after the kids for even one day will testify!) Busyness is one of the major obstacles to spreading the Gospel in Japan. From children to adults, the whole society is kept so busy that the average person cannot find the time or energy to hear the Word of God or to consider the claims of Christ. Busyness keeps people from reflecting on the meaning of life. This is especially true of the working men in Japan.

Missionaries and pastors also frequently get too busy. Striving to make the most of every opportunity to reach out to people with the Gospel, we often take on too much work. It is not just the meetings themselves that can cause overwork. The preparation needed to hold the meeting and to prepare a talk in Japanese takes much time and energy. Continuing language study also adds to the pressure. Sometimes we are motivated by a sense of urgency to get a church established and ready to call a Japanese pastor. It's even possible to be driven by a sense of competition or the desire to meet the perceived expectations of others. We constantly have to check our motives even as we work for the Lord.

To encourage spiritual and physical refreshment, the Mission was keen to find an inexpensive apartment where tired missionaries could go on their days off, just to get away from the pressure of work. We wanted a place that was within easy reach of Sapporo City so that it would not require a lengthy trip to get there, especially during the winter months.

Near where we lived, there was an area alongside the river with low-cost housing. The homes were built barrack-style with one unit adjoined to another in a strip of six adjoining bungalows. There were rows and rows of these simple homes filled with families. Visiting this site one day, I was surprised to find an empty unit at the end of a row, nearest to the river. "What a stroke of good fortune and blessing!" I thought. I wondered why no one had moved into this ideal spot.

Upon enquiry at the local municipal office, the rent sounded a little on the high side until the clerk went on to say the figure he was quoting was for twelve months. I could hardly believe my ears! The rent was ridiculously cheap! I signed the contract on behalf of OMF right away. I knew everyone would be really happy with the bargain!

The neighbors were curious that foreigners appeared to be moving into their area. Upon entering the apartment for the first time, the heavy scent of incense greeted me. Even the walls and ceilings smelled of incense. I opened all the windows and prayed in both of the rooms – a bedroom and a dining/sitting area that doubled as a kitchen. As I looked in the cupboards, I discovered some decorative Shinto arrows with white plumes. There were also some other Buddhist-looking items, which I put into a bag to take back to the municipal office. The clerk at the office was extremely reluctant to accept my bag, however. He went off and huddled with a more senior person, who came over to me with a concerned look on his face and insisted that I return all the objects to the apartment. By now I knew these objects were meant to offer some sort of protection, but I told the man that we were Christians and had no need of such articles. If they did not want them, I would throw them into the garbage. This called for another huddle of more important men, who kept glancing my way through the glass window as I waited at the enquiry counter.

Eventually, one man reluctantly accepted my bag of objects and very carefully stowed them away in his bottom drawer. He assured me they would be available to me should I change my mind later. I thanked him but said there would be no need, as Almighty God would care for us. In Japan, it is always best to attach a descriptive prefix when talking about God. The word *kami* (god) is used for both singular and plural in Japanese. When Japanese hear the word *kami*, they would immediately think of "the gods." A few weeks later I found out that someone had committed suicide in that apartment, which made it impossible to rent out because people feared the spirit of the deceased person.

The apartment was well used by various missionaries wanting a get-away for rest and refreshment. I also frequently used the apartment to get relief from my three lively children in order to get my Japanese sermon completed in time for Sunday. On hearing me leave the apartment one day, the lady who lived next door with a couple of children anxiously enquired if I had been disturbed at all. When I replied that I loved children and did not mind their noise, she waved her hands about to indicate that she was referring to spirits and such things, not her children! This presented another opportunity to share a testimony of God's care and protection of those who trust in Him. The people in this neighborhood needed to hear the Good News that would liberate them from their sin, superstition and fear of the spirits of their ancestors.

Around this time I had over-zealously tried to hit a home run during an inter-church softball game and had slipped a disc.

Doctor's orders were to rest and exercise slowly. One morning, when the children were at school and Pat had gone shopping, I had a strange experience. Lying down on my bed, feeling weak and sorry for myself, I suddenly heard a voice in my mind that said, "If you attempt to evangelize the people in the area near the river, I will touch your children." I felt a chill down my spine. There was no doubt in my mind that "touch" meant "harm." It was a threat from the Evil One! For a brief moment I considered the safety of our children as top priority. But then, faith brought me back to my senses – to trust completely in Jesus for every need, including the safety of my family. Besides, I knew that Satan does not keep promises. Praying aloud in my bedroom, I asked God to protect us from all evil, and to give us the strength we needed to penetrate Satan's domain. I never had a repetition of that voice again, but I knew we were in a spiritual battle for the salvation of those dear people who lived near our place of rest. We knew God wanted them to be brought into His Kingdom, so we proceeded with plans to reach out to them without fearing Satan. That dark threat reminded us that our strength and safety come from our Sovereign Lord. To be near to God is the best and most secure place anyone could be!

We began to visit and tract in the area, handing out Christian literature and invitations to special events at the church. No harm came to our children, apart from the normal spills from bicycles and falls at the nearby park where they played with the local children. Although I do not remember any significant breakthrough in the area, I was glad that the Lord brought us there to sow the first seeds of His Gospel as we witnessed to the people who lived alongside the river.

"When the servant of the man of God got up and went out early the next morning, an army with horses and chariots had surrounded the city. "Oh my lord what shall we do?" the servant asked. "Don't be afraid," the prophet answered. "Those who are with us are more than those who are with them." And Elisha prayed, "O Lord, open his eyes so that he may see." Then the Lord opened the servant's eyes, and he looked and saw the hills full of horses and chariots of fire all around Elisha." 2 Kings 6:15-17

As Christians today, we need to have that same vision and conviction to live faithfully without fear of the enemy or fear of people. Fear cripples. Faith strengthens.

"The Lord is the stronghold of my life - of whom shall I be afraid?"

10. THE VOICE FROM ABOVE

> *"In my distress I called to the Lord; I cried to my God for help.*
> *From his temple he heard my voice;*
> *my cry came before him into his ears."*
> - Psalm 18:6

Sapporo City on the north island of Hokkaido, Japan, has an annual snowfall average of six meters (twenty feet). *Hatsu yuki*, or the first snow of winter, often fell on my wife's birthday – October 17. I used to joke that God had sent her a birthday present. It was my job, however, to take care of the birthday wrappings – i.e. snow shoveling – which could last until late March/early April. Apart from the freezing cold, snowy white Sapporo has its own special beauty in the winter. During February each year, the population of two million swells, as visitors from many countries come to view the gigantic, innovative snow and ice sculptures at the annual Sapporo Snow Festival. Because of the enormous crowds, sightseers can only shuffle along slowly when viewing the many exhibits in downtown Sapporo.

It was just at that time of the year when a young man from Singapore came to Japan as a short-term worker. He was designated to spend a week with us to gain some insight and experience of church planting in Japan. We thought it would be a good idea for me to take Peter to see the Snow Festival; so we set forth, armed with his camera, ready to view something that was sure to be a first for a Singaporean!

There were crowds of people. The smell of roasted corn flavored with soy sauce, hot potatoes, and *amazake* (a sweet hot drink made from fermented rice) filled the air. People looked in wonder at the fantastic sculptures of famous buildings, cartoon characters, ice slides, etc. One particular sculpture caught Peter's eye. It was a small-scale replica of the Sydney Opera House. Peter told me he had been to the Opera House during a visit to Australia. As we walked along, we came to an elaborate ice carving of a church. Peter said he would take a quick photo from behind the building and then come right back. I waited in front of the building, making sure he could easily find me. That was the last I saw of my recently arrived, non-Japanese-speaking friend!

After several minutes had passed, I felt something must be wrong. However, I hesitated to leave my post in case he returned. As the minutes ticked by, it became obvious. Peter was lost in the crowd! I ventured to look behind the church sculpture, but there was no sign of him. His Chinese face blended in amongst all the Japanese faces, making it nearly impossible to spot him. I had lost a precious person the church in Singapore had sent to help us! I began to sweat despite the sub-zero temperature. Then I prayed fervently, confessing my oversight in letting Peter out of my sight. I should have known better! When you make a mistake, hindsight often seems to make you feel worse. How could I have been so thoughtless? I was no longer enjoying my visit to the wonderful Snow Festival. What should I do?

I made my way to the Public Announcement Office some distance away and asked them to call Peter to come to the PAO. The officials were not comfortable or willing to make an announcement in English. As Peter could not understand any Japanese, they asked me to make the announcement over the public address system in English.

Meanwhile, Peter was standing at the sculptured church praying earnestly that God would help us find each other. He realized just how lost he was. He had no name or address or telephone number to call. He was just totally lost! He too was sweating! While Peter was praying, a voice from above sounded in his ears. An English voice! The voice said, "Peter, this is Tony. Go to the Sydney Opera House. I will meet you there." To Peter, it was like the voice of God! The Lord had indeed answered his prayer.

I thought Peter would find the Opera House more easily than the church from which he had wandered away. As I made my way back to our rendezvous point, I was greatly relieved to find him waiting for me. Giving each other a big hug, we linked arms and enjoyed the rest of the time at the memorable Sapporo Snow Festival. I did not let him out of my sight again!

God always hears the prayers of His people. Too often we pray earnestly only when we are in trouble. What about praying enthusiastically and thankfully during the good times too? What better voice to hear than the Voice from above saying to His children, "I love you."

11. THE LORD OPENED HER HEART

> *"…one of those listening was a woman named Lydia …. The Lord opened her heart to respond to Paul's message".*
> - Acts 16:14

My wife and I have spent our entire 33 years in Japan working in various areas of Sapporo City. It is quite unusual for any missionary to have worked in only one city. Some of my more frank missionary friends have hinted that it was because I was unusual! (I am still pondering whether this was meant as a compliment or otherwise.) I like to think it may have to do with the fact that I was also engaged in administrative work in the Sapporo office for about a third of that time. At one point the mission – OMF International – designated us to the northwest side of Sapporo to begin a new church there. This meant starting from scratch, making contacts in the neighborhood and working out from there.

Having our children at the local Japanese school and daycare soon put us in touch with many people in our neighborhood. In no time we had a Sunday school of more than 30 children, mostly our children's friends or classmates from the local school. Our children's grasp of the language far outstripped that of their parents. Often I would consult their "wisdom" when preparing my weekly sermons. They told me my way of speaking Japanese was funny, which did nothing to encourage my flagging spirits. Mealtimes at home were in English in an attempt to keep the children speaking the language of their home country. But then the kids were usually quiet, trying to communicate with signals, coughs or foot taps under the table. Sometimes I would stretch out my foot to intercept a secret message from someone who wanted the jam on the other side of the table.

My wife, with her friendly smile, was also making contacts with people, offering to do Bible studies with anyone who showed interest. Some evenings I would go out taking tracts and knocking on doors to enquire if anyone would be interested to know the God who created them, as recorded in the Bible. Usually I would ring the doorbell and then take a step down to reduce my size so that I didn't project an overwhelming presence and frighten the occupant. I discovered that people sometimes kept the door open a bit longer when I did that. The great majority politely turned me down.

We decided to show Moody Science movies in our home for three weeks, followed each time by a short Bible talk. One day I went door-to-door in our neighborhood to invite people to the meetings. After numerous refusals, I was feeling discouraged, but pressed on to the next house.

When the door opened, a strongly-built man, clad in his undershirt, roughly asked me what I wanted and where I came from. Have I disturbed an important TV program, or does he think I'm just another Jehovah's Witness disturbing him, I wondered? (JW's are very active in Japan.) When I told him my country of origin, he angrily told me to return to apartheid South Africa. I felt anger rising up within me, but quickly decided I should exercise due caution, as he appeared to be in better shape than I was. Besides, OMF would not regard physical retaliation on my part as befitting a missionary who had come to share the love of God with the Japanese!

As I was considering my response, a strange thing happened. I felt as though a hand suddenly covered my mouth. I heard myself speaking to the man in a gentle, quiet voice. "What is happening?" I wondered, even while I heard myself speaking. It was my voice, but not my spirit, which was still a bit miffed. I heard myself saying quietly that I would be happy if he would come to my home, where we were showing Moody Science movies for three weeks, together with a short Bible talk. Then another strange thing took place. My former opponent spoke back to me in a kind voice, thanking me for inviting him. I began to feel that I would like to talk further with this man and become his friend. We parted on amicable terms. I continued knocking on doors, greatly encouraged, whilst making a mental note to ask the Lord about this event when I arrive in heaven.

Two houses down on the same street, a young lady opened the door and then stared at me in surprise for a few moments. Did my hair get messed up when I took off my cap or something? I wondered. Mrs. Noto listened to my invitation, expressed interest and promised to come. Many people make promises but do not follow through on them. Usually it is a polite way to get you to move on.

On the first evening of our event, the wind blew and rain came down in torrents. I retreated to a back room by myself to complain to the Lord. Although I had worked hard to invite people, He had not provided us with decent weather. Even a Christian might not venture out on a night like this! How were we supposed to get non-believers to come? I have often felt that God allows the opposition to appear to get the upper hand. When His people get pushed into a corner, into an apparently hopeless situation, God comes through in an amazing way to show that He is absolutely, always in control. The greatest example of this, of course, is the Cross and the Resurrection of our Lord Jesus.

Mrs. Noto did come to the meeting that night, together with a few other guests. In fact, every Sunday for the next two years, until the birth of her first baby, Mrs. Noto came to the Bible study/worship time. The Lord opened her heart and gave her faith. She was the first person to be baptized in the new church plant, and eventually became a pillar of the church.

Mrs. Noto told us that prior to my coming to her house that day, she had been in hospital. She had been walking past a downtown building one day when a piece of rubble fell on her head and caused a severe concussion. While she was in hospital, she wondered what would have happened to her if she had died. Is there a God? Is there a heaven? Where could she find answers? A day or so after her discharge from hospital, I came to her door inviting her and her husband to a Christian movie and Bible talk. Maybe this is where I will find answers, she thought, surprised that an "answer" had come so quickly!

Often we are not aware of how God is working in other people's lives. Sometimes we are even surprised at how He works in us! When the going gets tough, we may be tempted to give up. That's what Satan wants us to do. However, God wants us to persevere even when things look bleak and out of control. God wants us to walk in faith with Him, irrespective of any adverse circumstances. Mrs. Noto told us she felt that God had sent His messenger to her that day I came to her house. How close the messenger had come to giving up just two houses before hers! Satan had worked to discourage, but thanks be to God, who strengthens and encourages us!

Stay alert, dear Christian. You never know how God might use you as His messenger even when the prospects look bleak. A breakthrough to victory may be just around the corner if you do not give up!

12. UNFORGETTABLE BAPTISMS

> *"Therefore go and make disciples of all nations, baptizing them in the name of the Father and of the Son and of the Holy Spirit...."*
> - Matthew 28:19

Baptisms are always a highlight in the Christian Church. It is a time when a believer declares publicly that they have put their faith in the Lord Jesus Christ. Obeying Jesus' first command after putting one's faith in Him is also a significant first step for the new believer. Baptism signifies dying to self and rising to a new life with Jesus as Lord – a life of allowing Jesus, by His Holy Spirit, to live His life in and through the believer. In Japan, many Christians regard their baptismal date as the time they became a Christian. It is the time of burning their bridges behind them. For them and their family, the fact that they have become a Christian is now in writing. There can be no turning back.

Yasu, a teenage high school boy, had put his faith in Jesus as His Lord and Savior. Because the small one-storey house used as a church did not have a baptismal pool (the churches that OMF started usually practiced baptism by immersion), we used the bath at the nearby Alcoholics Rehabilitation Centre.

This work was started by OMF missionaries who were attending the church we were serving. Several men from the Alcoholics Rehabilitation Centre were also attending our Sunday services. I had to be extra careful to keep the messages short (which was no hardship, given my beginner's Japanese!), because towards the end of the service a certain amount of restlessness began to build up in those men, who were not used to sitting that long. Listening to a foreigner trying to speak Japanese in his first church plant must have made it even more difficult! As soon as the last "Amen" was sung, the men would dash outside for a smoke. Sometimes I wondered if the neighbors might have thought the church was on fire. Many times I did wish both I and the church were more on fire for God!

On the great day of Yasu's baptism, we all crowded into the A. R. C.'s bathroom, which could accommodate about six people in the bath. Daily it would be filled nearly to the top so one could sit submerged to the neck in the steaming hot water. There is no better place to be than in a Japanese bath during the cold winter months of Hokkaido! On the day of the baptism, the water was lukewarm. We were all standing in plastic slippers on the tiled floor of the bathroom, and people were pressed up tight to get a better view. Yasu was a young man of fairly heavy build, so when he got into the bath, sitting with his baptismal gown on, the water level rose quite a bit higher.

After pronouncing the baptismal blessing, I thrust Yasu backwards into the water but, to my consternation, I noticed that his face had not gone under the water. He was staring right back at me! Thinking that a half-baptism wouldn't do, and that Yasu deserved the full benefit of his baptism, I thrust him down again. The extra force was too much. The miniature tidal wave that burst over the side of the bath wall had everybody shouting in alarm and scurrying back into the safety of the passage as fast as they could. Unfortunately, not everyone could get out at the same time. Several observers were caught in the bottleneck at the door. It isn't easy to reverse wearing slippers that have no backs to them, so people were left standing in their wet socks as the water lapped round their feet.

Later, when the excitement had abated, someone mentioned that we had accomplished a foot-washing service as well as a baptism that day! Yasu survived his baptism and went on in his faith.

At another church I also witnessed an unforgettable baptism. It was held at one of the first churches established by OMF in Sapporo. This church had evolved from a Bible study for university students and had grown to include other members of the community. The church was a pre-fabricated temporary-looking building with a shallow, tin-lined baptismal pool. A missionary from another OMF church was borrowing the building to conduct a baptismal service. The missionary and the lanky baptismal candidate made a somewhat comical picture on this somber occasion, standing in water that only came up to their knees. Both the baptizer and the candidate appeared to be a long way above the water.

With a loud pronouncement the missionary rapidly lowered the candidate backwards into the water. There was a loud thud as the candidate's head struck the edge of the pool, followed by exclamations of "Oh!" and "*Ittai* (ouch)!" from the gathered congregation. The dripping wet candidate was raised to his feet, and assured the missionary and congregation that he was OK, though his eyes had a distinctly groggy look, much like a boxer who had just received a knockout punch! The missionary who had miscalculated the height of the candidate and the width of the pool went on to become a director of the Fellowship, which goes to show that some of our worst mistakes are not held against us forever. It really was a knockout baptism!

On another occasion, a missionary from another organization came to a small church in a rural village to conduct a baptism. It was winter time and three elderly people were due to be baptized. Missionary Mark was asked to conduct the baptisms, as the church was without a pastor. Being aware of the simplicity of the building and the severity of the cold in winter, Mark, with good foresight, brought his waterproof fishing pants and boots so that he would not get his suit trousers wet when he entered the baptismal pool.

Despite efforts to add hot water by kettles into the baptismal pool, they made little impact on the icy water, but it was pronounced acceptable by the three stalwart candidates. Older Christians always have something to teach younger, softer people through their example of coping with difficulties in life! In addition, rural people are often hardier than their city counterparts who have more amenities available to them.

Mark donned his fishing/baptismal outfit and proceeded first down the steps into the pool. The water was even a few degrees colder at the bottom than at the surface where it had been tested. Mark had to wait as each elderly candidate was helped down into the water and then up the steps and out of the pool before the next person slowly took their place. All the while, he was standing in the pool with a growing sensation that his feet were going numb because his boots were leaking! Each of the elderly people seemed to take ages getting in and out of the pool. Mark was beginning to feel glad that there were only three baptismal candidates that day! Normally he would have wished for many more. Following quickly on the heels (literally) of the last candidate, Mark climbed out of the pool to be greeted by another elderly person offering him a cup of hot *otcha*. *Otcha* is the green tea one initially receives at most places when visiting for pleasure or business.

By now our missionary felt his feet were in danger of frostbite, so without offering any explanation, he took one cup and then a second cup. Opening up his fishing pants, he poured the contents down his leggings to warm the water still in his boots. Then he did the same with the other leg. The completely flabbergasted granny found her voice and said, "*Sensei* (teacher), in Japan we **drink** the *otcha*. It is not for pouring down your trousers!"

The group of elderly stalwarts was not impressed with Mark's efforts to explain. However, after some fellowship and prayer around the kerosene heater in the church, everyone parted in good spirits, thanking the Lord for the wonderful baptism of three more people who had declared their faith in the Lord Jesus Christ.

Driving home without socks, Mark was grateful for the heater in his small car, but vowed that before the next baptism he would buy himself a new pair of fishing boots.

It had indeed been an unforgettable baptism!

13. GOD WORKS IN MYSTERIOUS WAYS

*If you had a hundred sheep, and one of them strayed away
and was lost in the wilderness, would you not leave the
ninety-nine others to go and search for the lost one until you found it?*
- Luke 15:4

On the day we moved into a nice, roomy house on the outskirts of Sapporo, Mrs. Horie, the lady across the road, kindly offered to help us move in. She also brought some drinks and snacks. Apart from our personal belongings, there was not too much to unpack or carry. We had to wait a few days for our larger items because we would be using the furniture of a missionary couple who were about to leave for their home assignment. In those days, furniture was pooled and used interchangeably as missionaries came and went. Little storage was necessary, as the furniture and appliances simply rotated from missionary to missionary. It was not a hardship to wait a few days to receive our furniture. After all, the Lord didn't even have a place to lay His weary head when He was on earth! I still have happy memories of our family of five picnicking on the floor eating Kentucky Fried Chicken.

The OMF Field Council had designated us to live in this area to start a new church. Our three children soon made friends with many children in the neighborhood, and their Japanese progressed in leaps and bounds. We never heard them argue in English until they were nearing their teenage years! On one occasion when my oldest son was about five or six, he said seriously, "Dad, why is Japanese so easy to speak and English so hard? I just have to open my mouth to speak Japanese, but I have to think hard before I can speak English." I looked down at this little guy and wondered if he was really my flesh and blood!

After a few months of introducing ourselves around the neighborhood, and a few initial outreach meetings, we started a Sunday worship service. At first just my wife and I attended. A few weeks later, young Mrs. Noto began to attend as well. During the first few months, there were just the three of us studying the book of John, singing songs and learning about prayer together. Mrs. Noto was drinking everything in and growing in her understanding of God's Word.

One Sunday morning during our little service, I looked up. Outside it was snowing; the sun was breaking through, and my heart was bursting with joy. If anyone had predicted that I would experience such joy and satisfaction with just my wife, one other lady and myself studying the Bible together, I would not have believed them. Surely a few more people attending would be more satisfying? But there I was, rejoicing in the presence of God, knowing I was doing what He wanted me to do. What could be more satisfying than that? This joy of doing church planting has remained with us through the years.

As the little group began to grow in numbers, I prepared sermons rather than just doing Bible studies. Mrs. Horie, the lady across the road, had offered to help me with my Japanese grammar and pronunciation. She was not a Christian so was not able to help theologically, but I tried my best to enable her to understand what I wanted to say. I would write my sermon by hand in Japanese (which was quite exhausting). Then I would take my sermon and read it to Mrs. Horie, together with the relevant Bible passage. She would then read it, make grammatical corrections and help me with difficult word pronunciation. Then I would read the corrected version back to her before returning home to practice again on my own. As the months went by, I was increasingly amazed at the way Mrs. Horie seemed to know just what I wanted to say. Often when I came home I said to my wife Pat, "Mrs. Horie seems to have a unique insight from the Lord to know what I intend to say in my sermon. It's incredible! She's not even a Christian!" Her questions and comments added spiritual value to the sermon as well.

Meanwhile, Mrs. Horie's two daughters, Yuri and Yuko, began to attend the English class we held before the worship service on Sundays. We always ended the English classes with one point from the Bible in Japanese, which appeared not to interest any of the students at all. It was quite discouraging. We would all laugh and talk together, seemingly the best of friends, but when we switched to Japanese Bible time, the atmosphere suddenly cooled. Sometimes I dreaded the last 15 minutes of our classes, but my wife and I always encouraged each other to continue, believing in the power of God's Word.

One Sunday Yuri and Yuko asked if they could sit in on the Sunday school class, which was sandwiched between the English class and worship service. They said they had no interest in Christianity but loved playing with children. We gave the two girls permission to attend. So it was that each week they attended both English class and Sunday school, helping and encouraging the children to listen to their teachers. The Holy Spirit warmed the hearts of these two "disinterested" girls, and they began to stay for the worship service as well. They became friends with other believers and enjoyed their Sundays at church.

In time, although their individual spiritual journeys took different turns, the Lord opened their eyes and blessed them with faith. Once they believed, they were eager to share their faith in Jesus with their parents. Mrs. Horie showed some interest, but not her husband, who steadfastly maintained he was a Buddhist.

One day Yuri and Yuko were shocked and surprised when their mother told them that she had been baptized as a Christian when she was 17 years old. She had later married their father, who was a firm Buddhist, so in order not to complicate their marriage, she had quietly put her faith aside. She had not read the Bible since then, nor had she ever told her children stories about Jesus. Initially the girls were really upset with their mother, but later only felt sad that she had denied the Lord and deprived them of a Christian upbringing. From then on, Mrs. Horie attended church occasionally when her husband was away.

Then I understood why she had insight into what I wanted to say in my sermons as she corrected them each week. Mrs. Horie told me later that she knew she was running away from God. "The day you moved in and told me you were Christians, I knew God was calling me back," she said. Directly opposite her kitchen window we had put up a sign in our garden, advertising the name of the church. She told us that every time she washed dishes and looked out the window, it was as if Jesus was standing there saying, "Mrs. Horie, when are you coming back to Me?" She had found it difficult to look out of the window while washing the dishes. Mrs. Horie did eventually come back to full faith and became a faithful member of the church. Sadly, her husband passed away without showing any interest.

As we reflected on the way God had led us to the house across from the Horie family, and the gracious and mysterious way in which He worked in their lives, we marveled afresh at the lengths to which God goes in order to bring just one wandering sheep back to Himself. God doesn't care how costly it may be to send a family from one side of the globe to the other in order to bring His truth to even one person. Cost is not an issue. After all, it cost Him the life of His only begotten Son to save you and me!

Yes, God works in mysterious ways. We may not know how, but what we do know is that He is always working. Who knows, He may already have begun a work of grace in the people who live across the road from you. Perhaps He is organizing events in order that His grace to them might be fulfilled through you! The Good Shepherd is always seeking His lost sheep.

14. EVEN A SHINTO PRIEST!

> *"For he has rescued us from the dominion of darkness and brought us into the kingdom of the Son he loves, in whom we have redemption, the forgiveness of sins."*
> - Colossians 1:13

Mr. Nakano, a professional man, was walking home from work one night when he spotted our church notice board advertising various meetings. Amongst all these activities, do they play *shoogi* (Japanese chess) at this place? he wondered. Just then the missionary in charge came out of the church to go home. They started to chat, and eventually the missionary invited Mr. Nakano to study the Bible with him. Mr. Nakano accepted, thinking, "It isn't quite what I was looking for, but it might be interesting". Although Mr. Nakano had never been to church before, he had read portions of the Bible, especially Revelation. He had many questions regarding the end times.

Over the months his interest grew, and he began to attend the Sunday morning services. That was where I first met Mr. Nakano. He started to bring his two young children with him to attend Sunday school, which met during the sermon time. In those days, sermons of less than 45 minutes were considered inadequate. The believers felt that, as they could only attend church on a Sunday, they wanted to make the most of the opportunity.

One Sunday before the sermon, when the children were present, the new worship leader forgot to announce for the congregation to be seated. We were all left standing while the worship leader was frantically studying his notes to see what was next on the Order of Service. The missionary's three-year-old daughter, who was sitting in the back row, shouted in Japanese, "*Osuwari kudasai* (please sit down)!" Relieved, everyone laughingly sat down.

Mr. Nakano continued to read the Bible with increasing understanding as the Holy Spirit worked in his heart. One day he announced that he believed in Jesus Christ and would accept Him as his Lord and Savior. His wife was really upset when he expressed his desire to be baptized as a Christian. She felt that he was betraying his own father, who was the Shinto priest at the local Shinto shrine. She vowed to oppose his new faith. Although she did attend his baptism, it was easy to see her antagonism, and she left immediately with no comment. Mr. Nakano's two children happily attended Sunday school each week, and he asked us all at the weekly prayer meetings to keep praying for his wife.

Meanwhile, Pat was reaching out to Mrs. Nakano, and she finally agreed to do a Bible study with her as long as no one told her husband! Then one day Mr. Nakano discovered that his wife was secretly reading the Bible at home, but being sworn to secrecy, we didn't tell him about the Bible study with Pat. Apparently Mrs. Nakano's interest was stimulated one day when she and the children sat down for their evening meal. The children said, "Mommy, we have to pray before we eat."

"Well, I don't know how to pray" she responded.

"Don't worry. Just fold your hands like this, and say the words after us. That's how we pray at Sunday school," the children said.

Mrs. Nakano later told Pat that after she had self-consciously repeated the prayer after her children, she felt her heart strangely moved. That incident had prompted her to agree to a Bible study.

Although she had been so antagonistic in the beginning, her interest in the Gospel increased rapidly. She still found it difficult to admit her interest to her husband, but eventually she too believed and was baptized, and she and her husband were united in Christ. God gave Mrs. Nakano the gift of evangelism – a gift that is much needed in the Japanese Church. She was always quick to share her faith with others, do Bible studies with them or invite them to church.

At Christmas time the small group of about fifteen believers decided to hold a "Family Christmas" in the local community center, and flyers were distributed to many homes. Mr. Nakano was to share his testimony. To everyone's joy, his father, the Shinto priest, also promised to come. We felt a little nervous, however, as to what to expect from him.

Shinto is an animistic religion of Japan and teaches that there are thousands of gods to meet the various needs of the people. There is a god for every occasion. Although Christians know there is only One True God, we should not discount the fact that some of these religions do have limited power over specific areas or events to influence people. Some people have experienced healing after praying to those "gods." Mr. Nakano's father's shrine was called the Shrine of the Snake and the family had experienced supernatural powers there.

The Family Christmas evening was a great success. The elderly Shinto priest seemed to be impressed with his son's testimony. He basically felt that all religions are part of one large spiritual family, so he was pleased his son's family had all become Christians, although disappointed that his son would now not be taking over his office as Shinto priest after him. He even offered to donate a tract of land to the church so that a suitable building could be erected. At the time the church was meeting in a small rented house, which was feeling increasingly cramped. The believers, however, turned down the offer, feeling it would not be wise to accept the gift before the priest bowed his knee before the One True Living God.

They continued to pray for his salvation, and although he was so open to hear the Gospel, he stopped short of putting his faith in Jesus Christ. He just could not see his need of a Savior – in his mind, he was not a sinner. After all, he had spent his life serving the community! However, after another man was appointed as his successor, Mr. Nakano Sr. began to attend church quite regularly with his family. Slowly his understanding grew and God blessed him with faith. At 92 he was baptized! Many Christians in Japan and other countries had been earnestly praying for the Shinto priest.

The new church building now stands on the land donated by him. God graciously rescued him and his family from the dominion of darkness and brought them into the Kingdom of the Son He loves, in whom we have redemption, the forgiveness of sins. All praise to Him!

15. A LITTLE HERE, A LITTLE THERE

> *"Always give yourselves fully to the work of the Lord, because you know that your labor in the Lord is not in vain."*
> - 1 Corinthians 15:58

White was not my favorite color during the cold Hokkaido winters! The snow keeps falling, day after day after day. "It's coming down. It's *still* coming down," we lamented every day. On one occasion, the snow on the roof of our house weighed so much that we couldn't open the front sliding door. I climbed out a back window to shovel the snow off the roof and away from the front door. Probably out of sympathy, looking at my tired face, one of my young sons said to me, "Daddy, ask God to make the snow go up." I agreed with his sentiments, but could not work up enough faith to ask God to take back some of His "blessings". Snow is a blessing to the skiers in winter, the farmers in summer, who benefit from the melting snow, and the fishers of trout in the flowing rivers.

During the long, cold Hokkaido winter, with temperatures sometimes dipping to minus 15 degrees centigrade, there was plenty of snow shoveling to do, not only at home and at the church, but also at the local bus stop. One time, due to physical tiredness sprinkled with perhaps a touch of procrastination, the snow had nearly swallowed up the church sign at the bus stop. Gritting my teeth against the wind and cold, I picked up my trusty shovel and set off, feeling like one of the early explorers to the North Pole. (Don't forget I am from South Africa!)

Several buses came and went before I had cleared enough snow to enable commuters to view the church sign to my satisfaction.

At that time, the church building was our home, for that's how OMF normally started churches in those days. There was no money available to rent a building suitable to be used as a church. Also, in the beginning of a church plant there were no or few believers, so initial offerings came from the only people present, who were the missionaries. Even when newcomers started to attend, we felt reluctant to pass around an offering bag before they showed signs of faith and were taught about the joy of giving to God's work.

A few days after clearing the church sign at the bus stop, I was sitting at the kitchen table reading my Bible and praying that God would send us some earnest seekers. I looked out the kitchen window facing the street and saw a lady walking in the snow. She appeared to be looking for an address. Perhaps she is looking for our church, I thought hopefully. I watched with disappointment as she walked on past our house and went to our neighbor's house. A few moments later she retraced her steps and disappeared.

A little later the phone rang. It was a lady enquiring as to the whereabouts of the church. She explained that she was not expecting the church to be just an ordinary house and, although there was a sign in the front garden, it was not clearly visible from the sidewalk because of the huge mounds of snow on either side. I promised to wait outside for her, and was pleasantly surprised to see that it was the same lady who had just walked past our house.

Mrs. Sato said that she had observed a man clearing the snow away from a church sign near the bus stop and wondered why he would go to all that trouble. "Why not just wait for spring to melt the snow? Why is it so important for people to see the church sign?" she wondered. So she felt drawn to look for that church.

After our initial contact and discussion, she soon became a serious seeker. We discovered that Mrs. Sato was a very intelligent and somewhat impatient lady. She found my Japanese reading and speaking ability too slow. She asked if she could read on ahead at home from the Bible and textbook. I was delighted! (God often used my weak Japanese to encourage others to do things themselves.) When we met each week, we discussed the areas that she had studied on her own but needed more explanation. Soon she also started to attend worship service on Sundays.

After a few months of diligent study, together with fellowship at church, Mrs. Sato was ready to receive Jesus as her Lord and Savior and committed her life to Him. She brought her son to Sunday school, but seemed to make no headway with her husband. He did not want to read the Bible, and usually fell asleep while she read the Bible aloud to him after retiring to bed each night. He also refused every invitation to come to special events at the church.

However, Mr. Sato liked to ski, so I arranged to meet him on the ski slope in an effort to strike up a friendship with him. He gave me some basic instructions on how to improve my rather laughable skiing ability, for which I was very grateful. My wife and I still laugh when we remember the funny sight I cut, slowly snow plowing down the hill with an anxious look on my face. Although skiing was fun, I was most happy when soaking in the bathtub at home, thanking God that I had not broken any limbs that day. Because of our friendship formed on the ski slope, Mr. Sato found it more difficult to refuse my invitations to come to special events at church.

The time came for us to take our furlough, or home assignment, as it is now called. We promised to pray for the Sato family. Several months later, we received the wonderful news that Mr. Sato had believed! Apparently, one day he just suddenly said to his wife, "I might as well come to church with you on Sundays," and it went from there. When we returned to Sapporo, we accepted their invitation to a meal in their home. Imagine our joy at hearing Mr. Sato offer a prayer of thanks for the meal and the salvation of his family! We sat with hearts full of thanks to God for His gracious work in their lives.

As we travelled home that night, I determined to be more zealous and energetic about keeping the church signs visible throughout the winters. You never know who, besides God, might be taking notice of what you are doing.

You see, our labor in the Lord is never in vain. A little here, a little there; it all adds up to something great when we are working with God!

16. LOOKING FOR THE RIGHT LOCATION

"It is fine to be zealous, provided the purpose is good…."
- Galatians 4:18

At one time, OMF regarded Hokkaido and Honshu (Tokyo, Sendai and Aomori Prefecture) administratively as one field under the supervision of a Field Director, Field Superintendent and Field Council. As Field Superintendent, I made periodic visits to our missionaries in all these areas. As a family man with a wife and three children, I felt like I was burning the candle at both ends at times. However, although there were often stressful matters to attend to, there were also many blessings. It was a privilege to listen to missionaries' stories and to pray with them for God's answers. Sometimes I observed missionaries getting so caught up in their work that their families suffered, but rarely did people get so involved with their families that the work suffered. Church planting was stressful at times, but we all shared in the joy when a church plant was handed over to a Japanese pastor, making it possible for a new church plant to be started elsewhere.

Such a time had arrived as we contemplated a new church plant in the Tokyo area. Missionary Andrew, a hard working "go-getter" type of person, offered to show me an area for a possible new work. It was getting late in the afternoon when we set out by car to take a look before the sun set. Andrew made use of every moment to achieve his goals so, considering his enthusiasm and the determined expression on his face I looked forward to the ride.

Tokyo streets are very narrow, so travel by car can be very slow at times. Andrew kept on taking "shortcuts," driving down secondary roads only to return later to our designated road, just one vehicle ahead of where we had been before. It did not seem to me to warrant all the gritting of teeth and tearing along even narrower back roads where people, cats, crows, cars and telephone poles were constant hazards. Dusk was falling. However, Andrew maintained we were making good progress.

It was getting darker as we left the congested traffic and headed towards a less populated area. Thinking we should soon arrive at our destination, Andrew surprised me by declaring that we were lost! Pouring over a map of a metropolis of some twenty plus million people is no easy task. We were out in a country area with no immediate help available. GPS's and cell phones had not been thought of in those days.

Just then a car went by. With a shout, "Aha!" we sped after the car, flashing our lights and honking in an effort to stop the driver to ask for directions. The car only went faster. Not to be outdone, Andrew went even faster! The man behind the wheel appeared terrified as we sped up a hill on the lonely stretch of road and drew alongside his car. Andrew was honking and gesturing for the driver to pull over. Instead, he sped even faster up the hill. Both vehicles were now going seriously over the speed limit! I had not helped the man to gain a good impression of us because I had pulled up my coat collar and slunk down in my seat in an effort to be less recognizable. I was wishing we could just come back the next day, but I was on a tight schedule and Andrew knew this was his only opportunity to show me this ideal location!

The frustration on Andrew's face and my own look of embarrassment were in stark contrast to the fearful look on the face of the man who, no doubt, thought he was going to be robbed by two foreigners. Although the man was now driving for his life,

Andrew, in a move that would have been the envy of any traffic policeman, expertly brought his car in front of the other car, slowing it down to a stop. Jumping out and rushing towards the man, now slumped over his steering wheel, Andrew showed him the map to ask directions. After a short time, he returned with a satisfied smile on his face. He now knew exactly where we were! We had not been horribly lost after all. We were just a little off track, he told me. As we drove off, I looked back. The man was still sitting where we had left him, even as we crested the hill. I hoped he was not having a heart attack!

We eventually arrived at our destination, where there were indeed many new high-rise buildings in process of completion. Soon these would be occupied by people moving further out into the suburbs of an over-crowded metropolis. Young couples with babies and small children were the ideal group to start a new church. Visiting in the parks, greeting people with a friendly smile, starting children's meetings and holding English classes would be some of many ways to make initial contact with people.

Already I could feel the excitement rising within me as I contemplated how the Lord might bring more people into His Kingdom. One of the joys of being a church planting missionary was seeing the Lord working in people's lives. My wife and I cannot think of a better way to spend one's life than bringing God's message of hope and salvation to people who have yet to believe. We only have to be there walking with Him, praying for His touch on people. I now understand a little better why Hudson Taylor, founder of the China Inland Mission (now known as OMF International) said, "If I had a thousand lives, China should have them. No! Not China, but Christ." Pat and I would say the same thing, except we would give them all to Japan, that the precious Japanese people might receive Jesus as their Lord and Savior.

Andrew had shown me a potentially wonderful location for a future church plant, so I made a few notes to bring to the Field Council. Andrew hoped he would be asked to work in that area and I knew he would definitely be a good choice. And if he did work there, he might even have an opportunity to bring the Good News to the driver we chased on the road that night!

17. YOU AND YOUR HOUSEHOLD

> *"Believe in the Lord Jesus, and you will be saved
> - you and your household."*
> - Acts 16:31

About ten people were gathering every week to worship the Lord in a rented house. The house was tucked away in a side street which was quite difficult to find even when you knew the address! We used to joke amongst ourselves that if the communists invaded Hokkaido, they would never find us. English classes with a 15-minute Chapel Time in Japanese brought us into contact with several young people who gradually began to attend church services. Having a nucleus of young people was great, and brought a lot of fun and laughter to the church.

One young lady, Junko, started to attend as a result of her involvement in a Black Gospel Choir. (Black Gospel has been a very popular singing genre in Japan for decades.) Junko wanted to understand the content of the songs, and was invited to come to church to learn more about the Bible. She was a gifted singer who enjoyed the company of the young people at church. She became a serious seeker and asked to be baptized. However, she had no concept of her own sin. She had often been the victim of ridicule and bullying, and could see the sins of others, but not her own.

Once during a short overseas trip, she found herself recoiling when a rather smelly man of another culture came to sit next to her on a bus. Junko was surprised and disappointed at her reaction, because she had always felt she treated all people equally, regardless of race or smell! Through this incident, God revealed her lack of love and innate sin nature in an unforgettable way. When she returned to Sapporo, she announced that she now knew she was a sinner in need of cleansing and forgiveness. She was ready to be baptized!

Junko's relationship with her younger sister Rina had always been bad. After her baptism, this began to change. Rina noticed that Junko was making an effort to be kind and inclusive, and she happily accepted Junko's invitation to accompany her to church. The fact that one of the believers gave Junko and Rina a ride to church every Sunday made their mother feel uncomfortable. She felt she should take care of her own family. So Mrs. Ogawa started driving her daughters to church. Then she decided to stay for the service instead of going home and returning later to pick them up. Although in her heart she had made the decision not to be influenced, she was also curious to find out what strange religion was captivating and influencing her daughters. Junko and Rina's change of attitude at home had impressed their mother, so she was ready to listen.

I remember Mrs. Ogawa sitting right in front of the pulpit in the small room, which had stretched to seat about twenty people plus a baby or two. At first it was quite intimidating to have her looking intently at me, showing no reaction on her face but obviously analyzing everything she heard.

I came to understand that she loved her husband and her children (she had four, which is quite unusual in Japan) and was concerned for the wellbeing of her family. She felt that her daughters becoming Christians would disrupt the family. Most Japanese practice ancestor worship because of a desire to preserve harmony amongst family members and relatives, together with a certain apprehension that trouble may arise from the spirits of the ancestors should they be neglectful of their duties at the Buddhist altar.

Meanwhile, the seeds of the Gospel were finding a place in Mrs. Ogawa's heart. Then one day she was hospitalized for emergency surgery. The believers all prayed that the surgery would be successful, and we and her children prayed for her every time we visited. (I have never known anyone to turn down an offer of prayer when they were sick!) Soon after she was discharged from hospital, she opened her heart and gave her life to Jesus. Although Mrs. Ogawa was clearly believing, she was reluctant to begin baptismal classes because she wanted her husband to believe and be baptized with her.

Mr. Ogawa did not appear to be the least bit interested. He was a hardworking businessman who carefully guarded his relationships with his business associates. He did not want to complicate matters by becoming a Christian and adopting different values and principles. Besides, Mr. Ogawa liked his *sake* (Japanese rice wine). He thought Christians were not allowed to drink alcohol, and used that as an excuse not to go to church with his wife. He was glad his daughters had become Christians, recognizing the new peace and joy they had. He was a little miffed, however, that his wife had believed, sensing it put a distance between them.

On one occasion when we held a men's cooking class, I invited Mr. Ogawa to attend. He said he would come if he were allowed to bring his beer with him. I said he could not drink in the church but what he did off the premises was his affair. Mr. Ogawa picked up on the idea and during the cooking class would go out to "check his car." His wife and several other ladies had volunteered to help with the clean-up after the meeting. They gathered in a room downstairs to pray for the men upstairs. Mr. Ogawa enjoyed the time and after that would occasionally turn up in church. I had a good relationship with him, but he remained stubbornly resistant to the Gospel.

Then Mr. Ogawa was transferred to another city. His wife and children remained in Sapporo until their tertiary education was completed. Later she joined her husband in the new location and started to attend a good church there. Mr. Ogawa began to accompany his wife to church more frequently, and faith began to grow in his heart as he listened to the Word of God. Miracle of miracles, Mr. Ogawa believed and was baptized! When I visited the church they attended, the pastor told me that in all his years as a pastor, he never had a person like Mr. Ogawa – he had invited more than thirty of his drinking companions and non-Christian friends to his baptism! He was not ashamed of his new Lord!

Since then, the Ogawas' second son and his wife have also believed and been baptized. Only the eldest son has not yet accepted Christ as Savior and Lord.

New Christians may feel lonely and regard themselves as the only Christian in their family or social circle. Our hearts go out to such people. We know they need a lot of encouragement to stand firm. We encourage them to see that they are not the **only** Christian in their family or circle of friends but the **first**. Others will follow, according to the promise of God: "Believe in the Lord Jesus, and you will be saved – you and your household."

18. TRUTH VERSUS HARMONY

> *"...grace and truth came through Jesus Christ."*
> \- John 1:17

"You will be disliked in Japan if you say Jesus is the only way." These were the words of Professor Yamamoto after one of the Japanese-language chapel times during the last fifteen minutes of our English class.

"That might be true," my wife said. "Jesus was disliked for saying that too!"

"You make Christianity too exclusive. Buddhism is not so narrow-minded," he continued. "We Buddhists accept all religions. That is better for harmony. We should be friends with everyone. "

This concept is held by many people throughout the world. Harmony versus truth – this is the battleground in Japan. Very few people care whether something is true or not. If there is a choice between harmony and truth, most Japanese would choose harmony. Perhaps if Paul knew the Japanese, he would say, "Jews demand miraculous signs and Greeks look for wisdom, *and Japanese seek harmony*. But we preach Christ crucified; a stumbling block to Jews *and Japanese*, and foolishness to Gentiles" (1 Corinthians 1:22).

We were always praying and looking out for seekers after truth. We wanted them to understand that true harmony is rooted in the harmony we can have with our Creator through Jesus Christ. Real harmony must be rooted in unchanging truth.

One thing that is frustrating for missionaries in Japan is that they have a wonderful message to tell, but very few people who are willing to listen. Making a connection with people to introduce them to the Gospel is very difficult. However, English classes provide a non-threatening and fun way of doing that.

Hiro first came to a high school English class at the church when he was 15 years old. Each student received a bilingual Gideon New Testament in Japanese and English. Hiro had never heard the Gospel before, and he listened with interest each week during the 15-minute Japanese chapel time at the end of the class. Later he started attending the special outreaches for young people at the church. The Holy Spirit began to use the Word of God, together with the warmth of Christian fellowship, to open his heart. Four years later, Hiro put his trust in Jesus.

Now, like a formidable mountain, the problem of telling his family that he wanted to be baptized loomed before him. "I know my father will be very angry with me for choosing a religion different from my family's" he said anxiously. Hiro's father was a strong Shinto believer. Shintoism is the belief in many local and national gods, who are credited by many people in Japan with having protected and prospered their country. Shinto teaches that the gods should be honored if that blessing is to continue. Besides, Hiro felt indebted to his parents because they were paying for his university education. He was grateful to his parents, and did not want to appear disrespectful by upsetting the harmony in his family. Harmony versus truth – he felt the conflict!

How and when could he tell his parents of his new-found faith? He sweated and prayed and shared his fears with me. I felt for him as a young believer on the brink of taking his first stand for Jesus in a society where to be different from others is not acceptable. In fact, holding to a set of values different from the group is seen as breaking the harmony of the group to which you belong – whatever that group may be.

Fellow believers encouraged Hiro and agreed to pray for him as he determined to try to talk to his father one Sunday night. Sunday night came and went, but Hiro chickened out. We told him that it would only become more difficult the longer he delayed. Hiro knew that was the case. He promised to try again the following Sunday night. However, when I contacted him on Monday, he said he did not raise the matter because the family atmosphere was not right. We all knew it would get harder and harder if he delayed again. The believers on the prayer chain prayed even more fervently that Hiro would be given the courage he needed.

On Tuesday evening, surprisingly, the whole family was together in the living room. Usually the TV would be on, his father would be reading the newspaper, his mother in the kitchen and his younger brother in his room doing his homework. That evening the family was just sitting quietly together in the living room! Hiro felt instinctively that this was his chance. He sent up a short prayer, took a deep breath, and started to talk about his faith in Jesus and his desire to be baptized. His father listened carefully, looking intently at Hiro all the time, but not saying a word until he finished speaking. How would his dad respond? Hiro was in for a shock.

When at last his father spoke, he said, "Hiro, if you are going to be a Christian, be sure to be a good one and not a half-hearted one." Hiro could hardly believe his ears! He was overjoyed at the wonderful way God had worked. He had had his first experience of stepping out on a limb for Jesus. He had stood for truth at the risk of harmony, but God had graciously brought truth and harmony together for him!

God blesses those who obey Him. It frequently takes more courage than we have, but God strengthens those who trust Him.

19. RUNNING INTO THE ARMS OF GOD

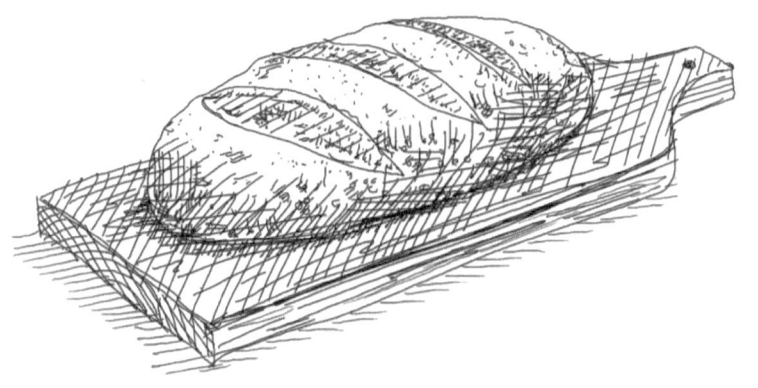

"Where can I go from your Spirit? Where can I flee from your presence? If I go up to the heavens, you are there; if I make my bed in the depths, you are there. If I rise on the wings of the dawn, if I settle on the far side of the sea, even there your hand will guide me, your right hand will hold me fast."
- Psalm 139:7-10

What would you do if your 21year-old son, an unbeliever, suddenly announced that he wanted to drop out of university at the end of his third year and asked you to support him so he could go to a big city to form a band? Most of us would probably say, "No way!"

Well, believer Mr. Uchimura carefully listened to his son's request to join a band in Tokyo. After some thought and prayer about his son's rebelliousness of late, he said yes to Taku's request. He would sponsor him for a year on one condition –Taku would have to agree to go to church every Sunday and attend a cell group each week for the next three months as preparation for living away from home. Although Taku was not keen on going to church, the condition did not seem too bad to him –three months of hardship in return for a year's financial support from his father! He hastily agreed.

So Taku started attending church. He sat in the back row, frequently looking at his watch and wondering how much longer he would have to endure. He also joined a mid-week small group meeting with several young people, but always left as quickly as he could at the end. However, during Taku's "endurance test" he found he was beginning to enjoy the companionship of his new friends at church and the small group meeting. Little did he know that God was working in his heart, both through His Word and through the warm fellowship of the believers. The Holy Spirit was giving him increasing understanding of his need for forgiveness through faith in Jesus, who died for him.

By God's amazing grace, Taku came to faith in Christ during those months. He could see now that going to Tokyo would not be the best option for him in his new faith, so he decided to stay in Sapporo and prepare for baptism. Taku was still having some issues at home, but relationships were improving. There was much joy and thankfulness at his baptism that summer! He did not feel inclined to go to Tokyo anymore. However, at Christmas time, as a result of a strong argument with his father, Taku suddenly left home without a trace. Much prayer was offered on his behalf, that God would keep him safe. Suicide always seems to be an option to some people, especially when they encounter very stressful personal relationships. Weeks went by, but there was no word of Taku.

Then one day he phoned home, intending to leave a message on the answering machine. To his surprise, his Dad answered the phone because he was home with flu that day. Taku gave no information as to where he was, just that he was safe. We were all so relieved!

Later Taku told us what happened. He had taken a plane to Tokyo (more than 1000 kilometers south of Sapporo), and then another plane to Okinawa (a further 2000 kilometers south). From there he took a ferry to a small, remote island on the perimeter of the Japanese archipelago. He was now about as far away as you could get from Sapporo and still be in Japan! Once he landed there, he knew he had to look for a job. He found a small bakery and asked if he could work there. The baker said, "Yes, on one condition – that you do Bible study with me every day before work, because I am a Christian."

Think of that! In a country where less than half of one percent of the population is Christian, what would be the odds of finding a Christian on this remote island? Taku was running away from his family, his church and God, but on this remote island he had run right into the arms of his Heavenly Father! It was as though the Lord said, "Hi Taku, I am waiting for you." What a wonderful God! What a wonderful demonstration of God's gracious, loving care for his immature, runaway sheep! We were all encouraged no end!

Taku studied the Bible with the baker and came back to the Lord. While he was there, he fell in love with a young lady in Okinawa. He brought her back to Sapporo, where she too came to know the Lord and was baptized.

At their wedding reception, Taku stood up before all the guests and asked his Dad to stand up too. Bowing low before him in front of everyone, he apologized for the trouble and anxiety he had caused his family and the church family. We, the guests at the wedding, truly felt the presence of God!

20. LOWER THE NET AGAIN!

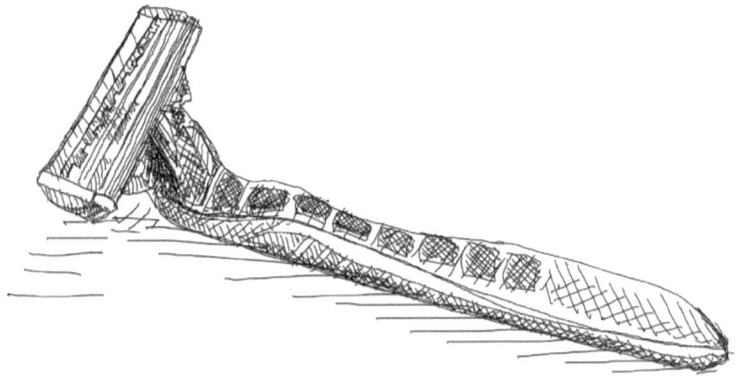

> *"… He called out to them, "Friends, haven't you any fish?" "No", they answered. He said, "Throw your net on the right side of the boat and you will find some." When they did, they were unable to haul the net in because of the large number of fish."*
> \- John 21:5-6

Mr. and Mrs. Kikawa, a middle-aged couple, started to attend our church occasionally. She said that she was a Christian but had not attended church for a long time. She did not evidence much spiritual life, nor was she keen to attend a class in order to transfer church membership. Apparently her previous church was no longer in existence. Although she was a Christian, we realized that she was not a good example to her non- Christian husband of what a Christian should be. We were glad, however, that they came to church with their daughter.

Mr. Kikawa often had to work on Sundays, which is not unusual in Japan, especially as the worldwide economic downturn was taking its toll. However, he came whenever he could, even when his wife did not come to church. With his interest growing, he had just begun a personal Bible study with us when he received notice from his company that, due to retrenchment, he was being laid off.

Now he was able to attend church every Sunday and any weekday he wanted to, but Mr. Kikawa began to retreat from making contact with people. Even though he lost his job through no fault of his own, he felt ashamed and redundant. He began to retreat to his room and only came out at night to go for walks alone. All attempts to reach him were unsuccessful. Whenever we called or popped around to visit, his wife tried to cover for him by saying that he was not available. In Japan this withdrawal condition is called *hikikomori*, which applies to people who, for various stress-related reasons, withdraw and hide themselves from society and ultimately even from their own families. Unfortunately this is a growing national concern for increasingly more people, both young and old.

About this time, the church planned to hold a second Alpha course. A big banner advertising the course was hung outside the church. Invitations were also distributed by way of flyers and personal invitations. We gave Mrs. Kikawa an invitation to give to her husband, but she said he probably would not attend. She confided that he was depressed, was not shaving, and had even begun to withdraw from his wife and precious little daughter, who loved her Dad so much.

A week before the Alpha course was due to begin, I had a nagging feeling that I should go and visit their home once more. However, I reasoned that there was not much point. I would only be making a nuisance of myself. His wife had told me she had urged him many times to attend. There was no charge to participate, so lack of finances would not be a problem. Still, the thought that I should try once more persisted. I felt a bit like Peter when he replied to the Lord that they had fished all night and caught nothing. What would be the point of lowering the net once more? The disciples "knew" there would be no fish!

Without much hope but feeling I should obey what was probably the prompting of the Holy Spirit, I set off in an attempt to personally invite Mr. Kikawa. His wife answered the door, but shook her head. She pointed upstairs to say that her husband was in, but he did not want to see anyone. "Please just tell him I would really like to see him briefly" I pleaded. Giving me a weary look which said, "It will do no good", she climbed the stairs and soon came down shaking her head, assuring me that he was not available.

In my heart I was just about to say to the Lord, "Lord, I told

You so. It was no use coming again!" when I heard a creaking noise on the stairs. Mr. Kikawa was slowly descending. He would not look at me. He hung his head, looking down at the floor. My heart went out to this man, who had just begun to taste and see that the Lord is good when disaster struck him. Speaking softly, I invited him to come even if only once, just to experience the course. "I'll come if I can", he said. This is usually a polite refusal in the Japanese culture.

Praying that God would bless the family, I slowly and sadly walked home. I realized Mr. Kikawa most likely would not come, but I felt encouraged to have connected with him again. I thanked the Lord for prompting me to go and persisting with me when I felt reluctant to obey.

On the first day of the Alpha course, just as we were about to begin, the door opened and in walked Mr. Kikawa! He still looked rather unkempt and avoided all eye contact with people. He just wanted to quietly observe without any involvement. We were overjoyed that he had come, even if only for this one time. However, the next week and every week thereafter, Mr. Kikawa attended the course! His whole appearance underwent a change as he shaved, dressed better, squared his shoulders and began looking people in the eye as he spoke. The Lord was healing his broken spirit and giving him hope again!

Mr. Kikawa was obviously enjoying the course and blossoming in the non-threatening fellowship he found with the three other participants. Towards the end of the course, with tears of joy and relief, he confessed Jesus as his Lord and Savior. Mr. Kikawa said he could not imagine that Jesus would consider him important, but he learned that with Jesus, even "A bruised reed He will not break" (Isaiah 42:3). He was so thankful that the Lord had persisted with him!

The day after the Alpha course ended, God gave Mr. Kikawa a job! Halleluyah! Unfortunately, that meant that he would have to be away from home for several months. But God nurtured and protected his faith. We later heard that Mr. Kikawa was due to be baptized. We were back in Canada on home assignment at the time, but on the day of his baptism we phoned the church and congratulated him, sharing in his joy!

As for me, I understood in a fresh way what Peter must have felt like when the net came up full of fish at the Lord's command. What blessings we may miss through trusting our own reasoning and not obeying the Lord. Lower the net again at God's command. He is able to do much more than we can ever dare to hope or dream.

21. A HAIR-RAISING JOURNEY

> *"Now to him who is able to do immeasurably more than all we ask or imagine, according to his power that is at work within us, to him be glory in the church and in Christ Jesus throughout all generations, for ever and ever! Amen."*
> - Ephesians 3:20-21

As a family we were facing a difficult choice. We had to make a decision that would radically affect our lives. Where would our children's tertiary education take place? Our daughter was finishing elementary schooling in Japanese and our two sons were nearing the end of English high school. This time, we knew we would have to stay in South Africa longer than the usual one year of Home Assignment in order to help our children adjust to life as young adults in South Africa. The trouble was that if we did that, political restrictions would prevent us from receiving a visa to re-enter Japan. It seemed that we would have to look into immigrating to a country that had good relations with Japan.

During our time of waiting on the Lord for guidance, the OMF Director for Canada visited Japan. He was actually staying with us, using our house as a base while in Sapporo. After he listened to our story, he generously suggested that he had a position in OMF Canada for us. We felt the Lord had shown us His plan for our family, so after further prayer we made the decision to apply for immigration to Canada.

So it was that at the end of a 5-year term in Japan, we set off to Canada via our beloved South Africa to say goodbye to precious family and friends there. Our three children were all teenagers then, and as was common in those days, OMF arranged for the most economical trip home for us. (That usually meant a roundabout way – direct flights were the most expensive.) Having received our tickets from the OMF office in Japan just a few days before our flight, we assumed the tickets needed no further confirmation. We set off on what was to be a hair-raising journey!

Our first flight was from Hokkaido to Tokyo and then from Tokyo to Taiwan. That was where our problems began. Apparently our flight to Taiwan had not been confirmed and that flight was full! They kindly put us on the next flight. However, that spelled disaster for a trip which had six connecting flights: Tokyo - Taipei - Bangkok - Karachi - Abu Dhabi - Nairobi - Johannesburg. Missing the first flight would jeopardize all the other connecting flights. We were devastated! As we sat together in the waiting lounge in Taipei, I said, "Let's ask God to delay the connecting flight in Bangkok so that we can make it." One of our sons said, "We can't ask God to do that for us – that would be selfish." "We can always ask," I replied, also feeling it was a bit of a nerve, but I couldn't think of another solution. "We can always ask and leave it with God, trusting Him to do what is right," I said. The family all thought that was a "theologically acceptable request," so we prayed while waiting in transit in Taipei.

Still feeling very anxious, we boarded a flight in Taipei bound for Bangkok, an hour late for the connection from Bangkok to Pakistan. When we arrived in Bangkok, a very flustered attendant was waiting at the door of the plane holding a sign saying, "Schmidt family, hurry! Baggage will follow." We ran down passages and through "officials only" doors and were quickly hustled onto a plane which had been kept waiting for us.

Angry glares greeted us as we boarded the plane. We didn't ask any questions but just meekly expressed our apologies, whilst filled with gratitude and amazement at the lengths God went to for His children! We felt bad for the other passengers on the plane, so it was difficult to rejoice aloud. We just accepted that

God had done what was right for us, His children. As we taxied down the runway for take-off, one of our sons, sitting a few seats back, whispered to us, "Dad, isn't God great!"

We successfully made our other flights, but unfortunately our luggage did not! Somewhere in the shuffle of planes all our checked-in luggage was lost. Unfortunately, our immigration papers for Canada were in one of those suitcases.

While waiting in Nairobi for a connecting flight, I tried to find out where our baggage was. "Don't worry, it will follow" was the reply. We had nothing except our carry-on bags. We settled down to a 17-hour wait in the lounge, as South Africans were "persona non grata" in Kenya at that time. The public address system was not working, so from time to time an official would appear to call passengers to board their particular flight. English wasn't his first language so we all had to listen carefully to figure out what destination was being announced. On one occasion the official kept on repeating agitatedly, "Kero, Kero". "Kero" is the sound a frog makes in Japanese! The kids couldn't help giggling. None of the passengers in the waiting lounge moved. The official grew hot under the collar, eventually asking people to show their tickets. Suddenly he started shouting at a man and demanded to know why he had not moved to board his flight when called. The passenger, along with some others, suddenly understood they had been called to board their flight to Cairo!

When we arrived in Johannesburg, exhausted by our three-day journey from Japan, we were still without our baggage. Each of the airlines involved denied any responsibility. I phoned them daily for ten days to ask about our baggage until an office secretary said sarcastically, "Mr. Schmidt, would you like to work for this airline?" Finally I was told the bags were in Nairobi but could not be released without the owner identifying the baggage personally!

However, a few days later a phone call came announcing the arrival of our luggage in Johannesburg. Once again we thanked our Lord for His mercy to us. Our immigration papers for Canada were still safe inside!

After a round of goodbyes to family, friends and country, we made it to Canada, where we were warmly welcomed by the OMF Canadian Director and his wife. Our children said, "Mom and Dad, we don't want to fly again for a long time - OK?" "Agreed!" replied their jet-lagged parents.

www.ingramcontent.com/pod-product-compliance
Lightning Source LLC
Chambersburg PA
CBHW020909080526
44589CB00011B/510